Leveling the Praying Field

Leveling the Praying Field

Can the Church We Love, Love Us Back?

ANSEL AUGUSTINE

ORBIS BOOKS

Maryknoll, New York 10545

The publishing arm of the Maryknoll Fathers and Brothers, Orbis seeks to explore the global dimensions of the Christian faith and mission, to invite dialogue with diverse cultures and religious traditions, and to serve the cause of reconciliation and peace. The books published reflect the views of their authors and do not represent the official position of the Maryknoll Society. To learn more about Orbis Books, please visit our website at www.orbisbooks.com.

Manufactured in the United States of America

Manuscript editing and typesetting by Joan Weber Laflamme.

Library of Congress Cataloging-in-Publication Data

Names: Augustine, Ansel, author.
Title: Leveling the praying field : can the church we love, love us back? / Ansel Augustine.
Identifiers: LCCN 2021035144 (print) | LCCN 2021035145 (ebook) | ISBN 9781626984509 (print) | ISBN 9781608339136 (ebook)
Subjects: LCSH: Race relations—Religious aspects—Catholic Church. | Racism—Religious aspects—Catholic Church. | Intergenerational relations—Religious aspects—Catholic Church. | Catholic Church—United States.
Classification: LCC BT734.2 .A54 2022 (print) | LCC BT734.2 (ebook) | DDC 277.30089—dc23
LC record available at https://lccn.loc.gov/2021035144
LC ebook record available at https://lccn.loc.gov/2021035145

Dedicated to the communities that shaped me:
New Orleans – Tremé
Fr. Michael Jacques, SSE
Sr. Eva Regina Martin, SSF
Fr. Jerome Ledoux, SVD
St. Peter Claver Catholic Church
and School Community (especially the youth)
IMANI TEAM OF NEW ORLEANS
HABARI GANI TEAM OF NEW ORLEANS
SANKOFA SOCIETY
Wild Tchoupitoulas & Chata Ogla Indian Tribes
All the ancestors, elders, young adults, and youth
who have fought, and continue to fight, for a just
society.

Contents

Part III
THE HOPE

Foreword

Fr. Bryan N. Massingale
Professor of Theology, Fordham University

I invite the reader to ponder these stories:

- I arrive at a suburban parish, whose members are overwhelmingly white, to celebrate mass for a priest who had suddenly taken sick. I ask the usher to direct me to the sacristy. He hesitates and asks, with suspicion, why I want to know. I explain the situation to him, thinking my visible Roman collar is already a complete explanation. He interrogates me, "You're a priest? Who sent you?" After replying "Yes," and explaining yet again, he responds, "Well, why didn't he send us a real priest?"

- It's the start of the new school term, and I arrive ahead of time to ready the classroom for my students. As the hour approaches for the start of class, the students start to get nervous, asking each other, "Where's the professor? When is the professor going to come?" This, despite the fact that I am standing in front writing on the board and am by far the eldest and most formally dressed person in the room.

To understand these narratives, you must know that I am a Black man, a priest, and a professor of ethics at a major Jesuit university in the United States. However, the only factor needed for full understanding is the pigment of my skin, my Blackness. Too often in America, it is the only thing that matters.

I know some readers will dismiss the racial interpretation I attach to these events (only two of thousands accumulated over 60+ years of life). They will say these are only "isolated incidents," or accuse me of "playing the race card" by alleging a nonexistent bias. And that is the problem. White Americans often refuse to acknowledge my experience. They minimize it, dismiss it, or even blame me for it: "What did you do to provoke such reactions?"

But note how white people assert the prerogative of determining what counts as legitimate evidence of white racial bias. You don't need a doctorate in ethics to see the inherent problem. Yet this conflict of interest remains opaque to most white people.

This is the core of the issue. America—and the Catholic Church in the United States—is constituted by a normative whiteness. Whiteness is the measure of who counts, whose experience matters, who belongs, who is accepted as one of "us," who is considered really "Catholic." And white people become the guardians of who gets to be included as one of "us."

Ansel calls his book "a love letter" to the church, a letter that bears a message of "tough love." He relates many stories like mine. Rest assured, there are many, many more from Black Catholics that go untold. Ansel's "love letter"—with its outcries, pleas, and protests—is but one of the many appeals that US Black Catholics have addressed to our fellow believers over the centuries. Appeals and protests that fall, for the most part, on deaf ears and stony hearts.

But readers should note that there is a dire consequence for this long legacy of rejection. In February 2021, the Pew Research Council published the most comprehensive survey of Black religious life in the nation.[1] Among its findings is that only a little more than half of Black adults who were raised as Catholic currently identify as members of the church. This is a far greater rate of attrition than is found in other communities. For example, over 60 percent of white adults raised as Catholic now remain. This is a dismaying reality, but one that frankly did not surprise me. Many Black Catholics know family members and friends who have left the church.

The report also provides the reasons for this steep decline. More than 75 percent of Black Catholics believe that opposition to racism is an essential part of what it means to be a Christian, yet only 13 percent of white Catholics feel the same. The survey also details the lack of attention to racism and the poor welcome that many Black Catholics experience in predominately white parishes. The bottom line is this: The Black exodus from the Catholic Church is due to a fundamental disconnect between what the vast majority of Black Catholics (and other Black Americans) see as essential for understanding faith and the concerns being addressed by most white congregations and white Catholic leaders.

---

[1] Pew Research Center, "Faith among Black Americans" (February 16, 2021).

The issue is not the white complexion of the Catholic Church's members. It is the unwillingness of the white Catholic community to engage realities that are existentially important for African American believers and Black Catholics.

This raises disturbing questions about US Catholicism and white Catholics. What kind of church are we if racial justice, practically speaking, is considered irrelevant or nonessential to being a disciple of Jesus? And how can the Catholic Church be what it says it is—"catholic" and universal—if almost half of its Black members abandon this church despite their high measures of religious commitment?

Ansel's book is a love letter that contains some hard truths. But he offers it with the same hope that has sustained Black Catholics through our journey in and with this church. We hope in the power of God who "makes a way out of no way." We trust that Jesus missions us to bring a difficult but vital message to our fellow believers. We hope that the Spirit, who "makes all things new," will use our work as catalysts for this church's radical conversion to the gospel. We trust that God can open the eyes of our fellow believers so that one day they will recognize the Real Presence of Christ in Black and Brown bodies.

We live in hope that when that day comes, then the Catholic Church will finally understand why we insist that Black Lives Matter. Because our lives are sacred, and our bodies bear the image of God.

We speak out, hoping that through our persistence, insistence, resilience, and perseverance, God will work a miracle, and make this church truly "catholic"—a place of welcome for people of every race, language, and way of life.

Introduction

On May 22, 2019, we celebrated our final school mass at St. Peter Claver Catholic School before closing after ninety-eight years of serving the Black Catholic community of New Orleans. This elementary/middle school has been an evangelical space where youth and families were able to grow in their faith. It was a safe space that molded many civil rights leaders, doctors, lawyers, and an array of public servants during its history. This space was a beacon of hope in New Orleans following Hurricane Katrina, after which it reopened as a central school that took in students from surrounding areas so that families, especially Black families, could move back knowing that there was a space where their children could get a good Catholic education that was grounded in culture.

This day marked the end of an era—when Black children could come to a school and learn about their faith from a Black perspective; where families could come to a school where they were taught about faith from a Black perspective; where Catholic school students, faculty, and staff would come into a school building with Catholic art featuring images of Jesus and other biblical figures that looked like the people in their school and community. As part of the uniform, the students wore vests made of kente cloth, a Ghanaian textile, made of handwoven cloth strips of silk and cotton. These images and uniforms sparked a sense of pride in our community. It also reminded those who attended, worked at, or entered our school, that they too are part of the salvation story. Many fear that our church might have the same fate in the near future.

Yes, there are still many other schools and churches around the country that continue to promote cultural understanding and awareness of their spiritual traditions, but they are too few and most of them are struggling to keep their doors open. Too many times, I, and others from my community, have had to "defend" our way of living our spiritual life as being genuinely Catholic, whether our artwork, our gospel music, or other culturally unique practices that may not be part of the usual Eurocentric worship at local and national gatherings. I have heard my brothers and sisters from the Hispanic/Latino community say the same thing, although some of their traditions are being more accepted by the church because of their growing numbers. Unfortunately, this lack of understanding and appreciation of our differences often points to the effects of racism within our church. Our safe spaces are diminishing and, often, the church hierarchy does not give its attention and resources to the issues affecting communities of color unless it deals with a public relations crisis.

Racism is nothing new in the church. In fact, Dr. Martin Luther King Jr., during his 1960 "Meet the Press" interview, said, "I think it is one of the greatest tragedies, one of the most shameful tragedies in America, that eleven o' clock on Sunday morning is one of the most, if not the most, segregated hours in Christian America." Racism is referred to as America's original sin. Just like human sin originated from the fall of Adam and Eve, so also many of the ills of division and injustice in America stem from racism. This racism originates in humans that make up the church. With the average American becoming "browner," due to various factors, it appears that white America is reacting to preserve an America where whiteness, and the values that come with it, are maintained; hence the popularity of the political slogan, "Make America Great Again."

So how does racism play out in our church today? As noted earlier, frequently church leaders don't address issues facing communities of color until they are forced to. Furthermore, racism is often at issue when people of color are only put in positions of authority in order to accept and promote values that promote Eurocentric ideals and values; when they challenge such ideals they are punished, ostracized, and labeled as "trouble-makers" or "antichurch." Thus, many national organizations that are created to serve communities of color are often so preoccupied promoting Eurocentric ideals in order to win over those in authority that they ignore the real needs of the people they are called to represent and serve.

There have been several church documents written about racism, especially in the Catholic Church, but whether they were written in 1979 or 2019, the same issues exist. It seems that the same events play out every time a racial incident happens locally or nationally: people are in shock; communities of color that are affected are terribly upset and start to take action; media attention brings the issue before those in church authority; some meetings, or gatherings, take place where people express their emotions; a church document is issued; some prayer services are held; and finally, things return to normal. There is no power shift or racial reconciliation where real issues are addressed, or people in authority—who may be part of the problem—removed. Thus, the cycle continues, and more people of color lose faith in the church—*especially our youth*.

Millennials (those born between 1981 and 1995) and Gen Z (those born between 1995 and 2010) are unique in that they have been shaped by the events of the world. In 2005, for example, the world witnessed my hometown flooded by the effects of Hurricane Katrina. The poverty of New Orleans was on full display to the world. So was the slowness of help to assist these expendable lives. And furthermore, across America, every year from 2014 on, there have been shootings by police of unarmed Black males including Trayvon Martin, Tamir Rice, and Michael Brown. Our youth have grown up seeing the media coverage of the murder of nine church members at Emanuel AME church in Charleston, South Carolina, by a white supremacist. These generations have witnessed the video of a white supremacist driving his car into a crowd of people protesting racism in Charlottesville, Virginia, injuring many and killing one. With the advent of social media these young people have been inundated with images and information dealing with a country and world that is still grappling with racism.

These generations have witnessed the rapid growth of hate groups throughout the past decade. They grew up under the message of "hope" under President Barack Obama, a president who faced many obstacles and insults that his white predecessors never faced, and some that came from the church itself. During the 2016 election, they witnessed the return of overt racism due to the effects of the previous presidential campaign, thus making it OK to say and do certain things toward others that were once taboo. Millennials and Gen Z are more social-justice oriented. Consider the many recent movements that have been formed and led by youth and young adults that we will discuss in this book. Many have left the church because of the hypocrisy when they hear that the church preaches one thing, but its members live by a different set of values.

To understand these generations, one must understand and appreciate their characteristics. According to a 2016 CARA study on diversity in the Catholic Church, 36 percent of parishes in the United States are culturally diverse,[1] a number that will only increase as time goes on. Forty percent of Catholics come from a Hispanic background compared to only 10 percent in the 1960s.[2] Fifty-six percent of nones (former Catholics), teens and young adults are non-white or multicultural.[3] Gen Z is majority non-white and the most diverse generation in US history, and they have more interactions with more diverse colleagues in person or through the internet.[4] Only 33 percent of Gen Z believe minorities have equal opportunities for success, compared to 43 percent of all other generations combined.[5] Seventy-two percent of Gen Z consider racial equality to be one of the most

---

[1] Center for Applied Reserach in the Apostolate (CARA), "Cultural Diversity in the Catholic Church in the United States," special report (October 2016).

[2] Hosffman Ospino, "The Church's Changing Face," *Our Sunday Visitor*, May 18, 2014.

[3] Robert J. McCarty and John M. Vitek, *Going Going Gone: The Dynamics of Disaffiliation in Young Catholics* (Winona, MN: St. Mary's Press, 2018).

[4] The Center for Generational Kinetics and Jason Dorsey, *iGEN'S Political and Civic Outlook*, The Center for Generational Kinetics, LLC., 2016.

[5] *iGEN'S Political and Civic Outlook.*

important issues today.[6] These stats indicate that "ministry as usual" from a Eurocentric perspective will not work.

Another challenge in addressing racism with the next generation is that, just as much as they are idealistic, they are also individualistic. In this era of social media it is important to help youth understand how addressing racism affects them and society. We, as a church, must remember not only to look at the systemic roots, causes, and effects of racism, but also at how our faith compels us to address this sin. We must not just teach *about* it, for this generation is asking us how we are going to act upon it to make a difference—otherwise known as "praying with our feet."

Despite all these changes in the demographics, most minorities still do not have the same opportunities as their white counterparts. This is known as the "unleveled playing field." This phrase takes into account that people of color do not make the same wages as their white counterparts and do not have the same access to safe housing, environmentally safe communities, appropriate education, job opportunities, wealth attainment, and a myriad of

---

[6] "The Power of Gen Z Influence: How the Pivotal Generation Is Affecting Market Spending," *Millennial Marketing* (January 2018).

other opportunities as their white counterparts. Even in dioceses across the country most of the attention and resources usually go toward churches or ministries that are in line with Eurocentric values, while many churches of color or ministries that serve them are underresourced, left to fend for themselves, and only receive attention during Black History Month or when holding special "diverse" liturgies. However, during these diverse liturgical events it has been my experience that any type of multicultural expression is seen as an entertaining sideshow and not an authentic expression of the faith. Many of those communities of color are not invited to be a part of the decision-making process in a diocese where policies and procedures may affect them negatively. At times, they may even feel like second-class citizens in a church that they, and their ancestors, have sacrificed so much to build. These and several other realities are what I refer to as the "unleveled *praying* field" in the church.

Millennials and the Gen Z generations see these issues and choose either to fight to create equality in the church they love or to leave. Unlike some of the older generations, they are not afraid to ask *why* when it comes to doctrine, policies, and, at times, lack of action on the part of the church, specifically on social justice issues. They are not afraid to speak out to bishops, priests, youth ministers, catechists, or other forms of authority, on issues that they feel need to be addressed to make the world a more just and "beloved kingdom." These generations see all global issues as just as important as what they may be facing in their own neighborhood. Their understanding of being one body takes on a whole new meaning in the age of modern technology.

These younger generations are inspired by Pope Francis because of his constant call for us to be church outside of our walls and to be a voice for the voiceless. It is our duty to make sure that we continue to examine our ministries in an ever-changing world. The message is the same, but the delivery has to change. How are we living out the walk of "accompaniment," as Pope Francis continues to challenge the church to do, with the young and those who are marginalized? When we talk about racism, do we refer to the past, when pictures were in black and white, or are we fearless enough to pull up recent social media posts that point out that it still exists today? Are we able to have frank conversations about institutional, environmental, and personal forms of racism that our communities face? Are we able to discuss the unearned privileges our community may have, and benefit from, that may unintentionally oppress others, and how we can rectify these situations?

These are the type of questions and reflections that our youth and young adults are thirsting for from our church. They want us to be prophets in a world that seems to be losing its moral ground. In a world where media constantly shows the disparity of life among people and the stereotypes that can be reinforced by such reports, our faith calls us to step out, be bold, and to challenge our society to conform to our faith values, not for us to conform to society's values. Our youth and young adults are drawn to those who are countercultural because they challenge the norms. Is that not what we preach when we speak about the life of Jesus? He was the most countercultural person that ever existed, and our youth and young adults are hungry to know about this man.

Yes, our parish school may have closed today, but my prayer is that what it represented in our community may live on through the youth and families that it served. It is institutions like St. Peter Claver Catholic School that have been the backbone that has supported and nurtured the faith for so many who may have otherwise been ignored. A faith that I believe Jesus called us to witness to the forgotten around the world. It is through Christ's inspiration that I write this love letter to the church. For if you love something, you will challenge it to live up to its full potential. It is through the hope of those I have met, been mentored by, and ministered alongside that I continue to uplift the future generations that continue to motivate me to keep pushing a church that sometimes chooses to ignore the voices of my community. Finally, it is though the power of my ancestors, who sacrificed much for me, that I now pave the way for those coming after me to make a more just society for others. It is time to level the *praying* field.

Part I

The Unleveled Praying Field

1

Studying Your Opponent

He has told you, O mortal, what is
   good;
   and what does the LORD require of
   you
but to do justice, and to love kindness,
   and to walk humbly with your God?

                              —MICAH 6:8

The Catholic Church in the United
States, primarily a white racist institution, has addressed itself primarily to
white society and is definitely a part of
that society. On the contrary, we feel
that her primary, though not exclusive
work, should be in the area of institutional, attitudinal and societal change.

                      —A STATEMENT OF THE
                      NBCCC, 1968

The 1968 statement from the National Black Catholic Clergy Caucus (NBCCC) could have been written today. In 1968, the NBCCC was looking at what it meant to be Black and Catholic in a world that had just experienced the assassination of Dr. Martin Luther King Jr. It was also grappling with racial unrest throughout the country as African Americans were fighting for civil rights and for recognition from the United States of their right to be treated with the same dignity that was afforded to white citizens of the country.

Just as the NBCCC was representing the African American Catholic community's place in society and in the church back in 1968, so too are we still trying to identify where we "belong" in our church today. This continues to be the struggle as we see continued challenges facing Black Catholics. Over the past several decades we have seen Black parishes, schools, and ministries that served as beacons of hope and evangelization in Black communities being closed. We have seen Offices of Black Catholics around the country being closed or often merged into Offices of Multicultural Ministries with the main focus being ministry to and with our Hispanic brothers and sisters with the Black Catholic needs being merely symbolic or an afterthought.

We have seen recent national movements from the United States Conference of Catholic Bishops (USCCB) focused on other cultural groups with little to no attention on the needs of the struggling Black Catholic community. We have seen the lack of attention on the right-to-life issues that affect the Black Catholic community (mass incarceration, gentrification, poverty, racism, and so on), with continued judgment and patronizing from various pro-life organizations because our communities are not as vocal about abortion issues as they think we should be due to our focus on trying to address these immediate issues affecting the survival of our communities.

We have seen many African American young men and women being rejected or traumatized by the treatment they have received in many of our seminaries and houses of religious formation due to the institutional racism that has made up some of the formation and the obstacles they face in trying to listen to God's call in their lives, thus eliminating pastoral leadership that benefits and can advocate for the Black Catholic communities. Furthermore, in diocesan staff around the country we see a lack of properly resourced Black Catholic leadership, thus increasing the inability for the church to connect with the needs of Black Catholic communities.

We have seen many of our youth and young adults labeled by church leadership with the same stereotypes that society has placed on Black youth, seeing them as disposable or problems to be dealt with, with no leadership qualities to contribute, or as needing to be "policed"/ controlled at diocesan events and gatherings, thus limiting the desire for Black Catholic youth and young adult ministries to want to attend such gatherings. We have seen our history and contributions to the Catholic Church—both internationally and locally—omitted or dismissed, thus creating the notion that we are "new" to the Catholic Church. We have seen many Catholic churches and campus ministries— both high school and college—unable to welcome new Black Catholics who challenge the Eurocentric norms in which they may have grown up in their home parishes. Often the reality of racism and how it affects the Black community does not get addressed unless there is a crisis that occurs, and thus we ask for a "kumbaya" moment without really dealing with the issues that separate us.

These are just some of the many factors that have created a division between the Black Catholic, specifically the African American Catholic community, and the church. In general use the term *leveling the playing field* refers to creating an environment of fairness. Although everyone is supposed to be playing by identical rules, there are factors that prevent some groups the same access to achieve the results that others may have. For example, in rugby one team may have an unfair advantage if its side of the field has a slope. So, to create "fairness," the teams switch sides at half time so that each team has an equal advantage and opportunity for success. Unfortunately, in our church this fairness has never officially been created. With all of the factors outlined above, along with many others that have not yet been mentioned, the church in the United States has become an unleveled *praying* field for many communities that are on the peripheries, as Pope Francis says. This book is not an attack on the church. Hopefully, it is a message of tough love for those who can, and want to, create change, to consider what needs to be done, and to affirm those who continue the fight for racial justice within the church.

The personal stories throughout this book are not offered to receive pity or praise but to share real-life examples of how the church has been complicit in the creating the reality we are experiencing today. There is much that needs to be said, and even more that needs to be done before true healing—leveling—can take place, but if we are truly people of faith, then we must continue to fight for justice and help to create the kingdom of heaven here on earth. *Let's begin leveling!*

The Game Plan

1. Where do you see racism in your local community (neighborhood, school, church, etc.)?
2. What do you see as causes and effects of racism in your local community?
3. Why does racism hurt all members of the community?

2

Proper Meal Prep

Man's creation by God 'in his own image' confers upon every human person an eminent dignity; it also postulates the fundamental equality of all human beings. For the Church, this equality, which is rooted in man's being, acquires the dimension of an altogether special brotherhood through the Incarnation of the Son of God. . . . In the Redemption effected by Jesus Christ the Church sees a further basis of the rights and duties of the human person. Hence every form of discrimination based on race . . . is absolutely unacceptable.

—PONTIFICAL COMMISSION ON
JUSTICE AND PEACE, *THE CHURCH AND RACISM:*
TOWARDS A MORE FRATERNAL SOCIETY, 1988

Let me take you briefly to my hometown of New Orleans, Louisiana. If you have ever visited this city, you know that it is one of the most unique cities in the world. In fact, many consider us the northernmost point of the Caribbean rather than a traditional American city. The combination of various cultures and traditions in the city's three-hundred-plus-year history has created a distinctive lifestyle that cannot be found anywhere else in the United States, although this way of life has been threatened due to the rapid gentrification following Hurricane Katrina.

Besides music, one of the greatest gifts that has come out of New Orleans is our culinary art. You would receive much skepticism from locals if you were to offer them any creole food outside of southern Louisiana. Certainly many of us are skeptical of local food cooked by someone we do not already know. I was blessed to call the late great chef, Mrs. Leah Chase, a mentor and member of my church family. She was a devout Catholic who attended our home parish, St. Peter Claver, faithfully with her family. She would allow me to use her family's restaurant, Dooky Chase, a famous civil rights location located in our neighborhood, Tremé, for various events with young people and their families throughout the years. The history of our neighborhood, Tremé, and Dooky Chase is significant. Tremé is the oldest Black neighborhood in the United States. It is where free people of color could buy land in the 1700s. It is where the civil rights movement is said to have gotten its spark from Homer Plessey (*Plessy vs. Ferguson*), a Black Catholic who attended St. Augustine Catholic Church, the oldest Black Catholic Church built by Black Catholics so the enslaved could worship in dignity. And, as already stated, it is home to Dooky Chase restaurant.

Dooky Chase is still a popular place, not only for its excellent food, but also because of what it has symbolized since it was established in 1941. During the era of Jim Crow segregation it was where Black musicians and politicians would enjoy fine dining when they were in town since they were not allowed to eat at the restaurants in the French Quarter. Also, the second floor is where many civil rights leaders would gather to meet and strategize how to create a more just society in New Orleans and beyond.

One of Ms. Leah's most famous dishes is her Creole gumbo. Her gumbo is known worldwide and is one of the most requested dishes when people come to the restaurant. In fact, on Holy Thursday people line up down the street to get a special taste of her own "Greens Gumbo," which has become a local Lenten tradition. I remember having to go to the back door to get a bowl for our former pastor, Fr. Michael Jacques. As Ms. Leah used to say frequently, many of life's problems can be fixed over a bowl of gumbo that.

It is over this bowl of gumbo I would like to offer another perspective about addressing the "original sin" of racism in America. Growing up, I remember hearing that America is the great melting pot, that no matter where someone comes from around the world, in America we all melt into one culture. The problem with this notion is that it erases and ignores the gifts of other cultures, unless they are Eurocentric, and forces immigrants, and those who may have been forced here generations ago, to forgo their own understandings and interactions with life and to adapt to a new way of being, thinking, and acting. This theory has, at times, caused many people of color to hate themselves and, in turn, to hate those from their own homeland, viewing their own culture and people as backward, insignificant, and inferior, unless that culture aligns with the American, mostly Eurocentric, ideal. In fact, some of the racist underpinnings of this ideology can be heard when we hear people challenging immigrants to speak English because this is America. This theory completely misses God's presence and wisdom that are expressed through various cultures. As research shows, millennials and Gen Z are being raised in the most diverse generations in the history of our country. It is no wonder that they are fighting outdated ways of interacting and values in America that limit the respect and dignity of others—especially in the form of racism.

Here I would like to present the "gumbo-pot theory," which is the opposite of the "melting-pot theory." A melting pot causes all the ingredients to dissolve into one new creation; thus the original ingredients are unidentifiable or cannot be traced. If you ever had a bowl of Ms. Leah's gumbo, you would see all the various ingredients clearly as you partake of the wonderful dish. You can clearly see the seafood—the crab and shrimp—in the bowl; you can identify the pieces of the okra and sausage; you can also see pieces of celery, onions, and bell peppers—New Orleans' "holy trinity" of cooking—as you lift your spoon out of the bowl.

The lesson in all of this is that the creator, in this case the chef, uses all the parts of these unique ingredients to create something wonderful and beneficial to all (unless you have a shellfish allergy like myself and need a special pot of gumbo). So too does God, our wonderful creator, use all our cultures to create the wonderful life and faith that we live out. The "gumbo-pot theory" means valuing one another's cultures as equally important to enhance our faith experience.

Unfortunately, this has been a challenge in the church. There have been many times that my community and I have been treated like second-class Catholics because of the color of our skin, the way we worship (Afro-Caribbean expressions during mass, gospel music, the environment, and so on), or the right-to-life issues that we prioritize in our communities (for example, mass incarceration, poverty, violence, and so forth).

The gumbo-pot theory presents a different perspective whereby we view each community's gifts and challenges as our own, no matter whether it is our lived experience or not. This can be seen in the third day of the African American celebration of Kwanzaa, when the principle of UJIMA (collective works and responsibility) is celebrated. UJIMA calls us to make our community's problems our problems and to solve them together.

How powerful would it be for the whole church to tackle all the problems together and not regulate them to some diocesan office or organization with limited resources? How impactful would it be for us to share resources equally among all parishes within the diocese so that all can have the same staff and opportunities to spread the gospel of Christ to those who need it most? What would be the long-term impact if all Catholic schools were given the same resources, no matter their location or demographics, so that all children have the same opportunities?

We have work to do in the church. The only way to level the *praying* field is to acknowledge our shortcomings and to make those important changes. So let's look at our own ministry environment and consider what ingredients or cultures (racial, socioeconomic, age, and so on) are missing or ignored and how to bring their voices to the forefront. It is only by doing this that we will truly be doing the work of God and encountering God in the lives of those who are different from us. In the following chapters I share some personal testimonies that illustrate how we are each called to raise awareness of the realities that occur within our institution that need leveling. This is not about me but about the work God is asking us to do within our communities.

The Game Plan

1. Why do you think it is important to learn about other people's stories/perspectives?
2. Whose perspectives are not included or heard, or are ignored in your local community (neighborhood, school, church, elsewhere)?
3. What can or needs to be done to include others' perspectives so that all can feel they are part of the community?

Part II

The Challenges

3

Knowing the State of Play

Racism can often be found in our hearts—in many cases placed there unwillingly or unknowingly by our upbringing and culture. As such, it can lead to thoughts and actions that we do not even see as racist, but nonetheless flow from the same prejudicial root. Racism can also be institutional, when practices or traditions are upheld that treat certain groups of people unjustly. The cumulative effects of personal sins of racism have led to social structures of injustice and violence that makes us all accomplices in racism.

—USCCB,
OPEN WIDE OUR HEARTS, 2018

One of the biggest issues in the Black, specifically African American, Catholic community is the lack of religious vocations. We hear about the varied vocations represented in the church—ordained, single, married, but when our church talks about vocations, it is really focusing on getting people into religious formation to become priests and religious.

Growing up, Fr. Michael Jacques, SSE (Fr. Mike), was a mentor, a father figure, and Sr. Eva Regina Martin, SSF, was a mother figure; both directed me toward a religious vocation. However, my heart was in music. But while I worked in radio and with various record labels in New Orleans, I was always connected to ministry in some way. I fell in love with youth ministry when Fr. Mike asked me to chaperone a lock-in at St. Peter Claver because they were short on male chaperones. That night changed my life's trajectory.

The young people I met were amazing. Many were younger siblings of friends that I had had for many years. After that night I started attending mass at St. Peter Claver more frequently and built relationships with these young folks and their families. Fr. Mike saw this and suggested I continue my education in ministry. It was by his suggestion, as well as Sr. Eva's, that I enrolled in

Loyola's Institute for Ministry and the Institute for Black Catholic Studies at Xavier University of Louisiana.

Being the youngest in both programs the idea of joining the seminary was often suggested by various people. I would tell them, "Who's gonna tell my girlfriend?" Nevertheless, I knew at that time that I was where God wanted me to be.

After Hurricane Katrina devastated my city in 2005, I lost nineteen people, lived in nine different cities, and had church youth and other family living in different parts of the country. It was not until 2007 that I was finally able to get a stable job with the Archdiocese of New Orleans and afford an apartment.

It was during this post-Katrina period that I contemplated my vocation and what God really wanted of me. Am I being called to be a priest? I had already lost everything, including several people that were close to me. So, before I decided to return to New Orleans, I applied to two religious orders to which I felt some connection. I was living away from home but was able to get all the information together for the applications in less than a week. (I could not even get my FEMA application done that quickly.) Surely, this was a sign of what God's plan was for me. I was excited, and so were the priests who were mentoring me from the first religious order. Unfortunately, the final decision makers thought the process was being rushed and suggested that I wait a year. I was not upset, but I assumed that this was not where God wanted me.

About a week after I got the news from the first religious order, the vocations director of the second religious order contacted me to inform me that he was coming to Texas, where I had been evacuated and was currently living, to meet with another applicant. He wanted to meet me over lunch while he was in town. He happened to be Vietnamese. We agreed on a time, date, and place to meet. When I walked into the restaurant and sat down to meet with the priest, the conversation was noticeably short and mostly uncomfortable. There was no sense of welcome or moving on with any process. I finally asked him, "Father, is everything OK?" He paused for a minute and responded, "I have to be honest; I don't think you have the look of a priest." I remember sitting there for about ten of the longest seconds that I could recall trying to fight back tears of anger, hurt, and shock. After expressing my anger—unfortunately, he received some of my pent-up Katrina aggression—I got up and left.

As the tears were flowing down my face, I walked past my car in the parking lot and into the street. I probably walked a quarter mile in the Texas heat with sweat and tears soaking my face and clothes. I thought about many of my conversations with priests, nuns, and various lay people about what they saw God was calling me to be. I thought about my many conversations with Fr. Mike and Sr. Eva about what they saw in me that I did not see in myself. I knew these people could not be wrong, but this "gatekeeper" simply said that my look prevented me from even going into seminary.

It was also during this period that I had some honest conversations with African American priests and seminarians about their horror stories during their times of studies and formation. Repeatedly I heard how some had to go through several different application processes with different orders just to get accepted. I heard, and continue to hear, how Black seminarians have to "play the game" and tone down their culture to get through seminary. I hear how many seminarians who have been subjugated to racism from seminary professors and other seminarians experience feelings of loneliness and depression that have led many to leave the process and the church.

Our church continues to "miss the mark" on Black vocations due to the internal racism that wants those in formation to become part of the melting-pot model rather than be authentic and unique according to our gumbo-pot model. There are many Black priests today who can relate stories of mistreatment and suppressed trauma from their seminary experience. It was in this call to a vocation experience that I, and many others, have felt abandoned and "motherless" by a church that claims that we are her children.

In 1989, Sr. Thea Bowman addressed the annual June meeting of the USCCB; she explained what it means to be Black (specifically African American) and Catholic. She said, "What does it mean to be Black and Catholic? It means that I come to my church fully functioning. That doesn't frighten you, does it? I come to my church fully functioning. I bring myself, my Black self, all that I am, all that I have, all that I hope to become, I bring my whole history, my traditions, my experience, my culture, my African American song and dance and gesture and movement and teaching and preaching and healing and responsibility as a gift to the church." She ended her moving presentation with the bishops standing hand in hand singing "We Shall Overcome."

Today, over thirty years later, we—as African American Catholics, and a distinct group of African, Caribbean, or Hispanics that identify as Black (often all lumped together as Black)—are still asking the church to see us as a gift and not a burden. Throughout our history as African American Catholics we have had to fend for ourselves in various ways. Our history, which is as old as the church itself, especially regarding the founding of the church here in America, is constantly overlooked and not shared. Our ministries are constantly underresourced or ignored. Our spirituality is constantly having to be defended as being authentically Catholic.

We are a people of great faith and achievements, but being a youth or young adult (including campus ministers) in the African American Catholic community is difficult. We constantly have to fight to find a place in a church that often treats us as though we do not belong. There are two factors that create this dynamic of marginalization: racism and proximity.

Racism

Racism, as we noted earlier, is commonly referred to as America's original sin. Out of that came the dynamic of slavery, the effects of which are still being felt today. It is this sin that makes it difficult to do youth ministry within the African American community. The USCCB's pastoral letter "Open Wide Our Hearts" attempts to address this sin and what the church should do about it as a follow up to the other pastoral letters on racism that the USCCB has written in the past. In addition to this letter, Fr. Bryan Massingale's book *Racial Justice and the Catholic Church* powerfully illustrates the issues that divide us as a church today, and Black Bishop Edward Braxton from the Diocese of Belleville in Illinois has written two strong pastoral letters about racism that many of his brother bishops have shared widely as well.

For those of us who do not have to deal with this issue on a regular basis, these documents remind us that racism does not only occur outside of the church, but that it is also a sin within the church itself that needs to be addressed. When we look at the history of our church in the United States, a Eurocentric model—in the styles of worship styles, the images used, and the languages spoken—is upheld as the norm, and in a society that is increasingly becoming more Brown, whether through immigration or births, there seems to be a growing backlash to anything that is not part of this norm. Look at the leadership of our chanceries around the country. Are the decision makers representative of the people whom they are called to serve? When people are called to the table to address racist actions, are all called, or does leadership only welcome those folks of color that represent the status quo and are seen as safe? Does our church blackball those who challenge these norms and label them as trouble-makers? When we have large diocesan or national gatherings of youth and young adults is the music that is played, the sacred images that are shown, and the speakers that are invited representative of the diversity of the church? Most of the times the answer is no. And, to add insult to injury, faces of color are often used as tokens to show diversity on brochures and marketing materials but not in the actual programming or decision-making process. It is these institutionalized racist occurrences that make African American youth and the young adult community feel excluded; we are called to do our own thing with little to no support from the wider church.

Proximity

In April 2018, as they were writing their pastoral letter, the USCCB invited Bryan Stevenson, a

famous criminal justice lawyer who gained recognition for creating the National Memorial for
Peace and Justice in Montgomery, Alabama—
more commonly referred to as the Lynching Memorial—to address its gathering on racism. During
his address Mr. Stevenson talked about several
factors that cause racism. One significant factor
is proximity. Proximity refers to how close things
are to each other. Mr. Stevenson said the issues of
racism persist in this country because people are
not within proximity of each other. We still live in
a segregated society. This is absolutely true of our
Catholic parishes around the country. Despite the
rise of many so-called multicultural parishes and
the existence currently of many distinct cultural
parishes, we are still divided as a church when it
comes to realizing the various expressions of our
Catholic faith and that no one expression is "more
Catholic" than another.

Bryan Stevenson indicates that one way to
combat racism is for those in leadership—bishops, diocesan leaders, Catholic event organizers,
liturgists, and so on—to be authentic witnesses.
When we were trying to rebuild the Archdiocese
in New Orleans following Hurricane Katrina, we
had many Catholic groups visit my home parish
of St. Peter Claver. These groups, most of whose

members were white and of various age groups, were in awe at our gospel choir and the sacred art that reflected the people in the pews. They were struck with the preaching that touched on the social justice issues that our communities face. Many were very appreciative of being able to sit with and interact with youth from the African American Catholic experience. When they learned about the specific right-to-life issues that affect our communities—such as mass incarceration, poverty, racism, poor education, and lack of resources— they understood that basic survival was a constant struggle for many of our families.

Just as Bryan Stevenson suggested to the US-CCB, it is when we are in proximity with one another that we can truly see the dignity of another human despite our differences. It is in this "sharing of space" that we share our souls and live as one body of Christ.

Similarly, when Sr. Thea began her talk with the bishops in 1989, she sang the Negro spiritual "Sometimes I Feel like a Motherless Child." In her presentation she continued to share the gifts that we, as African American Catholics, bring to the church, but yet how the church sometimes treats us as second-class Catholics because we express our Catholicism differently.

As African American Catholics we are simply asking the church that we love to love us back. Not only when it is comfortable and affirms Eurocentric norms, but when the church is challenged to be truly a welcoming church for all. Those of us who have worked in youth and young adult ministry within the African American Catholic community know all too well how we must tweak certain resources to be relevant to our youth and young adults' experiences. We know how sometimes we have to "fight" certain diocesan officials to help them understand we are just as Catholic as other parishes. We also have the challenge of helping our non-Catholic brothers and sisters understand why we remain Catholic. Today we are seeing various African American Catholic schools, parishes, and institutions close. We are also seeing our youth ministries dwindling. In conversations that are presently taking place between the USCCB and Catholic campus ministers of various HBCUs (historically Black colleges and universities), we are seeing the disconnect with many of our young adults and the Catholic faith. It was during a conversation with one of these campus ministers that the following questions arose. They are worth sharing here:

- What would it look like for national Catholic leaders and conference coordinators to attend our conferences (for example, the Archbishop Lyke Conference, the Institute for Black Catholic Studies at Xavier University of Louisiana, the National Black Catholic Congress) so they can meet the speakers and learn about those topics that are important to our communities?

- Would it be possible for these leaders to attend a Black Catholic gospel mass near them to explore ways of integrating our worship styles and environment into their diocesan and national events and not just use Black people as tokens?

- How can these leaders better connect with various organizations such as the NBCCC, the Black Catholic Sisters Conference, the Black Catholic Seminarians Association, the Knights and Ladies of Peter Claver, and the Black Catholic Theological Symposium and learn more about the histories of these organizations?

- How can we create more opportunities for diocesan and national leaders to come into "our" spaces so that they can understand our realities and needs?

These issues and the pain caused by having these constant discussions cause many who are doing this work to burn out or give up, but the hope is in the fact that our ancestors sacrificed much more so that we could be. We have historical records and stories passed down through the generations detailing their strong faith despite the disrespect they endured by the church. So, who are we not to do the same? Yes, it is a challenge to lift up the next generation of African American Catholic youth and young adult leadership, but it is a must. Our church has, and continues to benefit from, our gifts, but more work needs to be done to recognize our realities, needs, and worship experiences as valid and as Catholic as anyone else's. To truly be one means not to be the same but to be welcoming of all experiences and expressions of our Catholic faith.

The Game Plan

1. How do you think racism affects religious vocations in various cultural communities?
2. In response to Sr. Thea Bowman, what do you think needs to be done to see each other's uniqueness as a gift?

3. What suggestions do you have to move from conversation to action when it comes to addressing issues surrounding racism within your own local community (neighborhood, school, church, and elsewhere)?

4

Different Rules
for Different Players

Many times, the new face of racism
is the computer print-out, the graph
of profits and losses, the pink slip, the
nameless statistic. Today's racism flourishes in the triumph of private concern
over public responsibility, individual
success over social commitment, and
personal fulfillment over authentic compassion.

—USCCB,
BROTHERS AND SISTERS TO US,
1979

So, what were the challenges in leveling the *praying* field in New Orleans? Like many other dioceses around the country, most of the decision-making diocesan leadership in chanceries was, and still is, white. Even in dioceses with diverse population, many times outreach to ethnic cultural communities is relegated to various multicultural offices, if they exist, within that diocese, with the majority of other ministry focusing on middle- to upper-class European communities and those who may be connected to such communities.

This was the same problem in New Orleans, especially in youth ministry. In a very Black and Catholic city, there was some programming, but not enough, directed to a community that had more than twenty Black Catholic parishes, three Black Catholic high schools, and the only Black Catholic university in the country. Much of the programming that the Youth and Young Adult Ministry Office/CYO of the Archdiocese of New Orleans created was not relevant to the Black Catholic community there. It was not because the staff were doing this intentionally—many of them I still consider as friends and colleagues from that era—but it was because they did not know what they did not know as white people. They thought that their version of Catholic spirituality should work for everybody. There were pockets of programming for the Black Catholic community, programming that was being done by the communities themselves, but there was little interaction with the diocesan office regarding these initiatives.

My parish, St. Peter Claver, was one of the few Black Catholic parishes that would go to diocesan events, and usually I would have to send a letter to the CYO Office explaining why my youth and adult volunteers were either offended by something that was said from the stage or were upset that they were "policed" by the volunteer security that was there. This awarded me the label of a troublemaker by the CYO staff, and by some in the general youth ministry community, because I was challenging their values and was vocal about these issues at diocesan meetings.

In 2005, following Hurricane Katrina, we did our best to address these issues, since we were all in a transition period. After rebuilding my home parish and restarting our youth ministry program, I was hired by the CYO to work with our Black Catholic community in restarting our youth ministries and also to help diversify the programming of the office itself with the new staff that were working there.

My strategy was simple. I worked with the pastors, high school campus ministers, and youth ministers from our community to send students from our Black Catholic community to be members of the Diocesan Youth Board. This board was responsible for planning and implementing our large diocesan youth gatherings. The premise was simple: if we had more Black youth on the board, then the programming for these gatherings would be more relevant. Furthermore, we would be training future coaches to represent our community. It was our hope that as these youth graduated from high school, they would return to serve as adult coaches with the group.

Initially there was some skepticism from our community; some questioned whether they even wanted to participate. As with many of the Black Catholic communities around the country, the sentiment was, "Can we really trust the diocese?" This attitude stems from years of lies, lack of transparency, and even offensive comments and actions by diocesan staff and leadership and was very understandable. Nevertheless, our community bought into the program as long as the youth were there alongside me at the meetings, especially since the meetings were held at a church that was located in Jefferson Parish (*parish* is Louisiana's term for *county*), a predominantly white suburb outside New Orleans. So, for the first several meetings and with their parents' permission, I would pick up youth after school from our three Black Catholic high schools—St. Mary's Academy (all girls), Xavier Preparatory Academy (all girls), and St. Augustine High School (all boys)—and bring them to the meetings.

Over the next couple of years the number of members from our communities on the board surged: out of a total of 120 members, numbers of Black youth grew from five to nearly forty. This gave our youth a greater sense of belonging, as they had more people from their communities being part of this effort. Our representation of adult coaches from the Black Catholic community also grew. This helped me educate the white coaches on how to relate to the unique needs of our Black youth and the communities they represent. As more youth joined, their friends also wanted to participate. The pastors, youth, and campus ministers were pleased to see more Black representation in the form of people, culture, and spirituality at our diocesan events. It was a blessed moment in time.

Unfortunately, all that came to a screeching halt before one of the youth board meetings. As I stated before, we were meeting at a church in Jefferson Parish, an area outside of New Orleans. Jefferson Parish, especially this area of the suburb, is not a place frequented by Black people, but because this was one of the areas that had minimal effects from Hurricane Katrina and was available to host gatherings, the CYO was temporarily moved there until another space was located so that all the staff could be in one place. It was not uncommon for me to receive stares from drivers as I walked toward the parish office to attend staff meetings or to take care of other business while I was there. It was this same reasoning that led many of the Black families to want assurance from people that their children would be OK attending the youth board meetings at this parish. Everything was OK, for the most part, until this one event.

On Monday morning I received a call from my supervisor requesting that I come earlier than usual and open up the meeting center because our regular volunteer was going to be delayed at work. So, instead of picking up all the youth as usual, I just picked up the young men from St. Augustine High School. As we approached the center to set up the tables and chairs, a white lady appeared from around the corner and started to grill us with questions. She asked who we are, how we got the key, and why were we there. After pointing to my archdiocesan staff polo and their Catholic school uniforms, I informed her that we were there for the youth board meeting. At this point we were all on edge, because we felt that this woman did not have our best interests at heart. She then asked if the pastor knew we were supposed to be there. I sent the boys to go sit in my vehicle, and I then asked her who she was as I pulled out my phone to call my supervisor. Her immediate response, which made me freeze was, "I'm going to call the police."

My mind went to thinking of the safety of the young men and myself. Jefferson Parish police do not have the best reputation with Black males. I was concerned about what cops would arrive, who the police would believe, and whether we would make it out of this situation. I was very fearful and felt powerless as I tried to focus on what was best for the youth and myself in this situation. It was at that moment that several of the white youth board members and coaches showed up. The lady simply asked, "Are they with y'all?" When they responded yes, she walked away upset, as if she couldn't fathom why Black males would be at her church. The white coaches then turned to me and asked me who that was and what that was all about. I don't know if I was more infuriated at the lady's behavior or her assumption that we needed white people she did not know to vouch for our presence.

By this time the young men had called their parents, who came and picked up their sons. By the end of the night word had spread about what had happened throughout our Black Catholic youth ministry community, and we had to start to rebuild the numbers. Unfortunately, due to this incident the numbers never reached what they had been, but what is more hurtful is that my white colleagues failed to understand how all this was connected and why it was such a big issue.

In addition to this interaction, which was a major incident, and the many microaggressions that we faced from white youth and adults who were part of the youth board, older white coaches, and older CYO staff who belonged to the pre-Katrina system, I constantly felt the need to help these individuals understand the importance of Black expressions and that the culture and presence of Black people was not just valuable for entertainment purposes, but that we have gifts that they can learn from as well. The work continues to be exhausting with national Catholic organizations and colleagues throughout the country. That is why the various movements that have occurred throughout history to level various playing fields are so important.

Many of the grassroots movements in the history of our country that have called for systematic change have been seen as threats to the status quo because they were formed to transform and elevate the vulnerable and defenseless of society. Throughout the history of the world these movements have been labeled as radical and problematic by those in power. They have launched media campaigns and have directed resources to infiltrate, control, and destroy such organizations— with an intense focus on sullying the reputation of the leaders.

In the United States we have seen, especially in recent years with the declassification of documents from governmental security agencies, the targeting of civil rights leaders, the Black Panther Organization, the United Farm Workers labor union, as well as other race-based movements that have attempted to level the playing field. Catholics who support such movements are living out the premises of Catholic social teaching in their unique form of liberation theology. An issue that constantly arises is how police consistently make "mistakes" that have many times led to the death of unarmed Black citizens, yet they constantly manage to apprehend white citizens, even mass shooters, without killing them.

Does Black life matter? Our country continues to be at a crossroads with its "unfinished business" of race relations. Throughout the past several years the media have described the stories of several unarmed Black people killed by police. Either through blog comments or in regular discussions the opinions of who was at fault usually differs depending on the race of the individual speaking. Now, I don't want to put everyone into general categories, because not all people, Black or white, think the same way, but there have been general issues within various races that have led to the present state of affairs in the United States of America.

Writing through the lens of a youth minister from New Orleans, my city's issues with race and poverty were brought into focus during Hurricane Katrina. In the storm's aftermath the media revealed the racial divide through their reporting discrepancies that were often based on the race of whom they were reporting. For example, there were two Associated Press pictures of people wading through water with provisions under their arms. One caption described two white couples "after finding bread and soda from a local grocery store," and the other described a Black resident "looting a grocery store."[1]

This is the root of the problem in many race-related misunderstandings. There are two different Americas today—a white one and a Black (or minority) one. We see the reaction throughout the country to unarmed protesters grieving and enraged over the deaths of Michael Brown, Breonna Taylor, George Floyd, and hosts of other unarmed citizens at the hands of law enforcement. Law enforcement vastly overreacted to peaceful unarmed protesters, greeting those gathered for a candlelight vigil in full military/SWAT gear in some instances. In fact, many of these forceful reactions by law enforcement are what turned some of these protests into riots. As Martin Luther King Jr. once said, "A riot is the language of the unheard."

In contrast, in 2014 we saw a confrontation between supporters of cattle rancher Cliven Bundy and law enforcement at Bundy Ranch in Nevada that ended very differently with no shots or tear gas fired at Cliven Bundy and his armed supporters. We have even seen the confusion and delayed response to the majority white group of people

[1] Tania Ralli, "Who's a Looter? In Storm's Aftermath, Pictures Kick Up a Different Kind of Tempest," *New York Times*, September 5, 2005.

that stormed the US Capital Building on January 6, 2021. However, many of the scenes that have taken place with people of color—police with dogs, the signs held by frustrated protesters, the divide between law enforcement and protesters—are reminiscent of the civil rights era.

We might wonder why Michael Brown, an unarmed Black teenager, was gunned down in the streets of Ferguson, yet James Holmes, a white twenty-four-year-old who shot and killed twelve people and injured seventy others in a Colorado movie theater in 2012, was apprehended and treated humanely. We have witnessed countless white mass shooters who were apprehended without any violence. Police in Shelby, North Carolina, reportedly bought food from Burger King for twenty-one-year-old Dylann Roof after he was taken into custody approximately 250 miles northwest of Charleston following a sixteen-hour manhunt for shooting nine people in a church.[2]

There are many more examples of police brutality leading to the deaths of unarmed Black people: Eric Garner in New York City, Ezell Ford in Los Angeles, Sandra Bland in Texas, and John Crawford III in Ohio, just to name a few. There are also

---

[2] "Cops Bought Burger King for Dylann Roof Following His Arrest," abc7.com, June 23, 2015.

many other Black lives lost due to unnecessary police brutality in this country that do not receive news coverage.

Many of my white colleagues have asked, "Why are Black people so mad about this?" or "Why is this such a big deal?" Black people, and those who understand our situation, should not have to explain why it is not acceptable for unarmed citizens to be gunned down by the police, who are supposed to protect and serve, not judge and execute.

We should not have to agree with the statement that some make: "You all should just be less threatening or just comply." What was Martin Luther King Jr. wearing when he was shot? Does clothing automatically make someone a criminal?

We should not have to explain that the right of due process—which many of the unarmed Black men and women who were recently killed by police were not afforded—is in the Constitution—twice!

We should not have to explain why we fight back—a natural survival instinct—when unjustly attacked. We should not have to explain that many Black and other minority communities do not trust or have the same experience with law enforcement or the justice system due to past experiences of racial bias, intimidation, and the use of excessive force.

The actor Jesse Williams from the TV show "Grey's Anatomy" stated in an interview, "White people have the privilege of being treated like human beings." He noted that much of the anger in the Black community is fueled by the media's tendency—either guided by police reports or media bias—to make Black victims out to be "thugs worthy of their own death."[3]

Singer John Legend stated at a concert following the Michael Brown shooting, "One of our original sins in this country has been racism and slavery. And we still haven't figured out how to solve that problem."[4] This is the root of much of the anger in this country, and ignoring racism, and the fact that much of the privilege that many white people benefit from came at the expense and exploitation of other races, leads to situations like the one that we are facing now.

We are all made in the image and likeness of God. However, the excuse, "I don't see color," is not helpful because by not seeing my color, you do not acknowledge me. You do not acknowledge my

---

[3] "Jesse Williams on Ferguson: 'White People Have the Privilege of Being Treated like Human Beings,'" newsone. com, August 17, 2014.

[4] Gerrick D. Kennedy, "John Legend Teases Marvin Gaye Show, Talks Ferguson Unrest," *Baltimore Sun*, August 18, 2014.

history and culture. You do not acknowledge my race's daily struggles, nor the gifts and contributions that we have made to society.

This is also a reason why there is often a tension between the Catholic Church and Black communities; many times it seems the attention and resources of the church are not directed to our communities. There seems to be a disconnect with the issues we are dealing with, unless they become a public relations crisis within a certain diocese.

God calls us to care for all of our brothers and sisters. Pope Francis has challenged the church—and the whole world—to look out for the needs of others, especially those most in need. The silence of many of our church leaders on issues of racism is hurtful to many, and for the church to be an entity that truly values the "dignity of the human person," we must be vocal on all issues that threaten human life.

We, as a people of faith, are challenged to look at racism, poverty, and injustice as right-to-life issues. Just as we are adamant about fighting abortion, we must fight to make life safe and just after the child is born. Is this not what Jesus wants of us? This is the time for us to practice our faith. God is speaking through these situations. Are we listening?

It is never easy to talk about racism. But we all do talk about it within our own racial groups. It is something that affects us all, either directly or indirectly. We, especially the Catholic Church, need to be able to share our hurts and challenges. People who benefit from society's current social structures and institutions may not see the necessity of addressing this issue, but as long as one part of the body of Christ is affected, we all are. Only when we truly challenge the norms that may cause divisions (on both sides) will we be able to come together as the loving church that we were created to be. We must put aside our stereotypes and fears and look at one another as brothers and sisters made in the image of God.

So, what can we do?

- *Do not ignore what's going on.* The silence by many leaders is speaking volumes. Not saying anything or not praying about injustice publicly gives the impression that it is not a big deal.

- *Admit that there is a problem.* These Black men and women did not deserve to die the way that they did. The justice system is broken. In many cases law enforcement got away with murdering unarmed citizens that posed no threat. That is unjust.

- *Know that this is an issue that affects the whole body of Christ.* For some, especially those who cannot relate to the victims of these deaths, this is just another news story. But for many others—especially those of us in the African American community—it is more than that. These stories of unarmed people being murdered by law enforcement are familiar stories, a story that repeats itself throughout history. In Michael Brown, George Floyd, and other victims, we see a son, a husband, a father, a nephew, a youth ministry kid, and even ourselves. As church folk, we need to reach out and listen, mourn together, and try to understand with the community, not theorize, judge, or assume.

- *Continue to express Christ's love to those who are suffering and bring justice to those who are lost.* It is time for us to be church and not just talk church. This is an opportunity for us to show others how Christians step up in the face of unjust attacks.

Let me be clear, I know that the cops who did these hurtful acts are not representative of all police officers. I know that there are many officers who truly live out their motto to protect and serve. I have many friends, and youth ministry kids, who are cops, and they risk their lives on the streets of New Orleans to uphold the law by working with, not threatening, the communities they serve. But there is a broken system when certain people are allowed to abuse their authority and certain communities who should feel safe and protected live in fear and distrust.

So, does Black life matter? It should, because this is one of the right-to-life issues our church is called to address.

The Game Plan

1. What challenges do you see in your local community (neighborhood, school, church, and elsewhere) in authentically including people from various backgrounds into the community?
2. What can be done in your local community to make sure that people of various backgrounds feel equally valued and included?
3. What can institutions (media, law enforcement, and civic and church leaders) do to avoid the stereotypes that they sometimes display or uphold?

5

Valuing All Players

Each of us as Catholics must acknowledge a share in the mistakes and sins of
the past. Many of us have been prisoners
of fear and prejudice. We have preached
the Gospel while closing our eyes to the
racism it condemns. We have allowed
conformity to social pressures to replace
compliance with social justice.

—USCCB,
BROTHERS AND SISTERS TO US,
1979

What comes to mind when you hear the term "anti-Blackness"? Is it images of lynchings throughout American history? Is it movies about slaves that you may have seen? Is it archival images of people reacting to the integration of schools or civil rights protests from the past? These are all accurate and form part of what we are dealing with when we talk about anti-Blackness.

What is more sinister and dubious, however, is how our systems, including the institution of our church, buys into this philosophy. When I speak of anti-Blackness, I am talking about society's disregard—even disgust—for anything connected to Blackness (culture, rituals, traditions, wisdom, history, and so on) unless it benefits the values of and norms of the status quo. This means, in other words, that society can accept Blackness as long as it is entertaining (music, sports, and so forth) but will deny it if it challenges Eurocentric norms as a whole (social justice protests, history that contradicts Western thought and ideas, spiritual practices, and the like). So far, I have shared some personal testimonies that form the basis of this concept.

My ministerial journey advocates for all the youth in my community, not just the ones accepted by society because they affirm Eurocentric ideals.

Frequently, I and other youth ministers from the Black Catholic community have observed how diocesan and national youth ministry offices and organizations will latch on to the Black youth that is "polished," "well spoken," or may be considering a religious vocation. They will promote this young person prominently at their events and in publications to showcase their Black Catholic youth who "fits" their ideal of a good Catholic. What then happens is a "brain and talent drain" from our own communities. Usually such young persons become so involved with these diocesan and national groups they are no longer connected to their own community. These are the same communities that sacrificed for these young people to achieve such dreams from which these white organizations are now benefiting. Thus, we are left, as always, ministering to the 99 percent of the youth who are seen as irrelevant, or debased, because they do not abide by the same white-leaning norms and thus make these institutions feel uncomfortable. In other words, their presence at these diocesan and national gatherings often challenges the Catholic norms and programming that these organizations adhere to and offer. This was the challenge I had to address when we were integrating the diocesan youth board for the Archdiocese of New Orleans following Hurricane Katrina.

What has saddened me the most is that anti-Blackness can be found not only in other races but even among some Black people as they achieve class mobility in this country. It is a reality that is many times perpetuated in our church and continues to affect the most vulnerable in our society. It is a problem that is hardly ever addressed but is ever present and always felt.

In 2012, I met a certain priest of Hispanic descent. We became good friends and stayed in contact on a regular basis. Whenever I would visit his area of the country, I would be sure to reach out and visit him. He would do the same whenever he was in my area.

This relationship changed when the topic of race came up. He had grown up in a more privileged situation and found Black culture fascinating and even used some of our cultural aspects whenever he presented to youth, but he struggled to understand, or even see the value of, the struggle for social justice within our community.

This is where the initial tension between us emerged. I would confront him about using the "n-word" around me, which was a common custom in his close circle of friends, most of whom were

Hispanic. We ended up arguing about why certain demographic groups could not just adapt to the status quo and how those of us who were fighting for a more just society were just acting spoiled and were ungrateful for what we had. Unfortunately, I had to end our friendship after calling him out on his hypocrisy. He used his influence and privilege as a priest to ostracize me from various youth group communities with which we were affiliated. What was most upsetting about this were the opportunities that were blocked for my youth and youth ministers.

I realize that his attitude is not reflective of most Hispanic and Latino people in ministry, and I have many friends and colleagues who are part of that ministry. However, the fact remains that a good amount of attention and resources are dedicated to our Hispanic/Latino brothers and sisters in our church, whereas the members of the Black Catholic community, which has been here since the founding of the church in this country, have often been treated as second-class Catholics. I recall, for example, a time when I was turned down for a position because it was assumed that I did not have enough Hispanic experience, even though they never asked about it, nor did they research the work I did with Hispanic young adults through the campus ministry work I had done. Yet the same organization called me to assist it in drafting its antiracism statement, organizing other Black Catholics to connect with and develop resources after the murder of George Floyd.

This is the same issue many Black Catholics face around the country. We are ignored until we are "needed." Our contributions are seen as inauthentic unless they benefit the status quo and, many times, we are used as the "spiritual black-face" to deflect, or even bear the brunt of, any negative racial issues caused by past indifference and ignorance by these organizations.

"Black Is Beautiful! Black Is Beautiful! Black Is Beautiful!" This is the mantra that I had the audience shout during my panel presentation at the Convocation of Catholic Leaders in 2017. I received much praise from the Black participants, but many of the white participants, who formed the majority of the conference, took offense at this "exercise." Most of the participants were diocesan staff and leadership from around the country, many of whom were and still are overwhelmingly white. The discussion during this plenary session was about ministering to people on the peripheries, those that are forgotten or overlooked.

Too many times in this country, and yes, even in our church, Black people, especially African Americans, are forgotten and overlooked. It is usually not until November (Black Catholic History Month), or February (Black History Month), or when there is a racial PR crisis that attention is given to Black communities and issues within specific dioceses. Furthermore, those of us who have been working in Black Catholic youth/young adult ministry have had to, and still have to, "fight" to get the wider church to understand the unique needs of our communities.

Too many times throughout the history of our church, especially in the United States, the term *black* has a negative connotation. Let us take for instance the controversy surrounding the phrase *Black Lives Matter.* For many Black people this phrase is used to remind folks of the unequal treatment of Black people throughout the history of this country as well as the present realities that institutional racism creates within our communities. Many in church leadership have connected the meaning of the phrase to the organization that carries a certain political agenda, but most of us are using the phrase not to promote the organization, but so that the church might pay attention to the needs of one of its original communities that is continually pushed to the peripheries. This "distraction ploy" used by many in the church to avoid addressing the meaning behind the phrase is also similar to other tactics used to ignore America's "original sin" of racism . . . and thus the problem continues.

It will be through hard dialogue (even though many of us are exhausted from talking about this issue) and the sharing of power and resources that this issue will be tackled, not through more letters and statements. It will be through the building of authentic, mutual relationships that this issue will be addressed, not through "savior mentalities" where certain groups come in to "fix" a community.

At this moment I ask those reading this to take a long look at where you can address America's "original sin"—within yourself, your family, your community, your church, your school—and how you can learn to create a more just world so that we can see Blackness as a gift as Sr. Thea Bowman told the bishops in 1989. Let us move forward as people of faith to create a world where Black lives are beautiful!

The Game Plan

1. Where have you seen anti-Blackness in society or in your own local community (neighborhood, school, church, elsewhere)?

2. Are there other groups that you see being marginalized, or discriminated against, in your local community?

3. How do you think America's "original sin" of racism has affected American society both in the past and today?

6

Playing against Stereotypes

For this reason, "every offense against the dignity of man is an offense against God himself, in whose image man is made." This dignity is common to all, without exception, since all have been created in the image of God. Jesus's answer to the question "Who is my neighbor?" demands of each individual an attitude of respect for the dignity of others and of real concern for them, even if they are strangers or enemies. In all parts of America, the awareness that human rights must be respected has increased in recent times, yet much still remains to be done, if we consider the violations of the rights of persons and groups still taking place on the continent.

—JOHN PAUL II, ECCLESIA IN AMERICA, 1999

In 2016, I was invited to be one of the keynote speakers for the Youth Day at the Los Angeles Religious Education Congress in Anaheim, California. As I usually do with any speaking engagement, I wanted to showcase some Black culture as a learning opportunity for those who might not regularly be exposed to such content. Since this was a large gathering, I chose to do a similar type of cultural expression to that I had done for my keynote presentation at the National Catholic Youth Conference (NCYC) in 2013—stepping. For this presentation not only did I tie this Black cultural art form into our worship experience and use it as a form of prayer, I also used the opportunity to educate those in the audience on what stepping was and its sacred significance for the Black community. I specifically did not want to present this cultural expression as a form of entertainment, for that would have detracted from the primary importance of the art form.

I have used stepping three times as part of my ministry presentations—twice for the NCYC and once for the Youth Day in Anaheim. For both of the National Catholic Youth Conferences, I used high school youth from New Orleans who were already planning to attend the conference. In the months prior to the conferences, I aimed to educate them about the history and importance of stepping. As with the keynote presentations themselves, I taught them the origins of stepping in the African gumboot dance used by miners and how it is now used by Black fraternities and sororities across America as an expression of their ancestral traditions. It has been my hope that my speaking engagements would be an opportunity for those in attendance to learn about the sacredness of my culture and its various expressions, and not just be a form of entertainment.

For the Youth Day event in Anaheim I was blessed to receive a grant from the National Black Catholic Congress that sponsored some of my young adults, who had formerly been a part of my youth ministry and were now mentoring some of the youth in the Archdiocese of New Orleans, to attend. Most of them were already accustomed to stepping because they were part of a Black fraternity or sorority when they were in college. Therefore, I did not have to educate them about the sacredness of what we were about to do. We just had to practice—and practice we did. Every Sunday afternoon for months we would gather at one of our parish gyms and practice for hours until we got the routine set. We were even running through the routine after we arrived in California.

During the dress rehearsal we realized, to our dismay, that the stage was carpeted. This muted the stomping sounds that came from our feet. Consequently, we had to stomp harder. We did the routine twice for the repeated keynotes that day. The young people and their adult chaperones turned my young adults into superstars that day. It was a blessing to watch my young adults being asked about their faith, hearing their responses, and being asked to pose for pictures with the attendees.

That afternoon I was invited to a gathering of youth ministers in a suite and was asked to bring the step team with me. When we entered the room, we realized that we were the only nonwhite people there. We all gathered in one corner when it was time to begin the program for the afternoon. There was even a group from Australia present!

The host of the gathering suggested we go around and introduce ourselves, and after a moment of awkward silence, someone suggested that my step team should start. So, one by one, my step team members introduced themselves by stating their names, their home parish in the Archdiocese of New Orleans, and their occupation. As the members stated their occupations—chemist, accountant, engineer, pharmacist, graphic designer,

FEMA team member, college admissions counselor, banker, office business manager—many of the white people looked stunned. After each introduction there was an, "Oh, wow," "Oh, my God, that's amazing," or some other response that made it apparent that several of the white people in the room could not believe that the members of my step team, who were all Black, were capable of holding such positions. It was apparent that the stereotypes they had in their heads—or their limited interactions with Black people—were very much on display at that moment.

When I saw how this was playing out, I said that we had somewhere that we had to be and did not stay for the rest of the program. Of course, as we were riding on the elevator, all the team expressed how uncomfortable they felt during that experience.

Unfortunately, this is the predominant lived reality of being a Black Catholic. There is a duality of experiences, and we constantly have to "prove" that we deserve to exist in certain Catholic spaces. Due to the bias in the history that is taught, the theologies that are upheld, and even the vestiges of slavery and Jim Crow, being "made in the image and likeness of God" seems only to refer to whiteness in our church. This painful reality is expressed through the stories of various elders, priests, religious, deacons, lay church workers, and even when you talk to young Black adults who struggle to stay in the church.

Since many diocesan and church decision makers do not have authentic relationships or experiences with any communities of color, they rely on the stereotypes that are presented about these communities, and their policies and practices in relating to these communities are often based on these stereotypes. These long-upheld stereotypes have plagued the relationships between races within the church. Thus, the divisions continue. This reality is the "elephant in the room" when we talk about the real pro-life issues in various communities. It is the reality when "ideal candidates" are discussed for diocesan leadership roles. It is often the reality in what the church deems as holy and as sinful at various conferences and in some church publications.

The result is that the church and these communities become disconnected, especially today, when we look at the mass exodus of our African American Catholic young adults from the Catholic Church. This is a result of generations of neglect—and the problem is that the church as a whole really does not seem to care until there is a PR crisis relating to race. Then it resorts to a series of listening sessions, statements, and symbolic prayer services that are futile, especially with this age group.

The White Savior Complex

In addition to the stereotypes, another issue that causes even more friction in trying to level the *praying* field is the "white savior complex." In fact, both of these issues deem people of color, mostly Black people, as unable to be their authentic selves or to solve issues in their own way. Both issues diminish the power, wisdom, cultural norms, and other aspects of these communities as inferior or needing the assistance of white people and Eurocentric norms and wisdom to "fix" their communities.

White savior complex describes the mindset of white-led institutions or individuals who help nonwhite people in a manner that benefits and prioritizes whiteness. Faith-based racism and the white savior complex go hand in hand by wrongfully using religion as a tool to exploit historically oppressed populations. Missionary charity work by white faith-based institutions toward nonwhite populations is an example of this complex that validates white privilege through faith.

I have encountered these "white saviors" in various dioceses, national Catholic organizations, and youth and campus ministries. The white savior complex is never really about justice but rather about maintaining the status quo. Sometimes this approach is intentional; other times it stems from a mindset inherent in the society in which the individuals have been raised and taught about white values versus the values of other communities. What is frustrating for me and many of my colleagues of color is when we hear ministry leaders say, "I see no color," or "My community is not racist," or "I love everyone the same," or even "Jesus does not want us to be angry or upset," when it comes to dealing with issues of race, diversity, and inclusion. They are willing to have a symbolic "kumbaya moment" but will not really address the problems at hand.

What this is communicating to us is that such a person does not value our communities' experiences, wisdom, and unique traits, but more important, that this person does not really want to address the needs of our community. Furthermore, this tactic is a distraction from dealing with the issues of diversity and racism, and thus an option to maintain the status quo.

The white savior complex through faith-based racism is evident within the structure of the church throughout the country where white administrators in the ministry have ostracized valid concerns of racism from various communities of color to coopt marginalized experiences and center white voices to address nonwhite injustices. An example of this is when I worked in predominately white institutions, including various dioceses or universities, that were trying to deal with diversity or racial issues. They would center the conversations and work on "helping" or "saving" those in need, but they would seek to control the communities they were attempting to engage. Many times they would ask people of color from the organization (parish leaders, students, and so on) to be part of the process, but those in control of directing the conversations and work would be white or people who would not challenge those in control. The people of color who are part of the work usually do not have any decision-making power and are usually used as "props" to prove that the white organizations are authentic and connected to the struggles of the people, or communities, with whom they were trying to connect. Unfortunately, this process causes damage to the communities that they are coming into and to the people of color who are being used because it often pits these groups against each other. In effect, the white people involved usually "feel good" and those of color still have to deal with additional trauma caused by this process. I have seen this with many well-intentioned nonprofits, Catholic and otherwise, that do social justice work with communities of color where their leadership (board of directors and staff) is predominately white.

These entities have always portrayed themselves as benevolent, humanitarian efforts to "fix" the problems of people of color. The problem, however, is that these people have the same mindset as the people who caused and continue to cause the issues that these communities face (theft, colonization, exploitation, genocide/extinction, enslavement, and so on). These groups profess that they want to solve the problems their communities caused but still benefit from them. The white savior complex is just slavery and colonialism in another form. In other words, whiteness and its values are kept at the center rather than really addressing the problems of communities of color. Therefore, power is not shifted, resources are not shared, and only those people of color that adhere to these values are allowed to be heard. Consequently, the problems persist and there is little authentic change.

We can see this lack of change clearly, for example, in the church documents on racism, specifically the USCCB documents "What We Have Seen and Heard" and "Brothers and Sisters to Us," both written over fifty years ago. They discuss the same problems that communities of color are still facing today. What has changed? Who are the decision makers? Who is being silenced? Who is leaving the discussion? Does church leadership really challenge the status quo and create effective and authentic change? What needs to be done to help young adult Black Catholics who are leaving the church to feel welcomed and feel that the church cares about what matters to them?

These are the tough questions that need to be addressed before we can truly level the *praying* field today.

The Game Plan

1. What stereotypes do you see upheld in your local community (neighborhood, school, church, elsewhere) and how are these harmful?

2. How do you see the white savior complex affecting your community, or other communities, around you?

3. What biases or stereotypes do you hold about others, and how can you try to change your perspectives?

Part III

The Hope

7

Teammates on the Praying Field

All of us are in need of personal, on-going conversion. Our churches and our civic and social institutions are in need of ongoing reform. If racism is confronted by addressing its causes and the injustice it produces, then healing can occur.

—USCCB,
Open Wide Our Hearts,
2018

What does it mean to be a true ally—supporter and advocate—on the *praying* field? Let me be clear, this book is not a condemnation of white people, but rather an attack on white supremacy and all its vestiges, especially those, in the church and beyond, that have caused much trauma in communities of Black Catholics, especially within youth and young adult ministries. The personal stories that I have shared provide some concrete examples of how the "original sin" of racism has affected Black Catholic youth ministers as well as the youth and young adults they serve, and prevents them from feeling fully accepted and included by the church. The stories serve as a challenge to those who do not realize there is an issue, do not want to acknowledge there is an issue, or do not know how to address an issue that is not their lived reality. They also serve as a reminder and an affirmation for those "fighting the good fight" to continue to advocate for our youth and young adults to remain connected to a church that often does not see them as fully functioning humans due to the misconstrued values of our society.

This ongoing fight is why it is important to have allies in the work of leveling the *praying* field and to create racial justice within the church. An ally is usually a person, often from a privileged identity group, who stands *against* oppression and stands *for* the liberation of oppressed communities whose concerns are usually ignored or dismissed. Allies support the ideas and directions presented by oppressed groups rather than making decisions on behalf of the group—something that would merely represent/reinforce the current system of power and privilege. In various ministry settings I have too often had to deal with white colleagues who want to control how to *solve* racism rather than *listen* to the challenges of those affected by America's "original sin." Being an ally does not make someone an expert. Having a Black friend, being married to a person of color, adopting kids of color, or living in a diverse neighborhood does not make a white person an expert on speaking about, speaking for, or fixing the issues that those communities face. This is just another form of colonization where the history, needs, and gifts of the community are wiped out and replaced with the needs of the white people. This is happening across the country in Black and Brown neighborhoods where we are experiencing the ever-increasing reality of gentrification.

My own neighborhood of Tremé—the oldest Black neighborhood in the United States—became gentrified following Hurricane Katrina. Longtime

Black residents could not afford their homes any-more due to property values increasing when new residents, mostly white, came in and bought up houses. Even today we are fighting to express our unique culture that once made our neighborhood so attractive. Now the white residents who have moved in are threatening the culture that shaped the community because they are finding the large musical gatherings inconvenient. This reality is also threatening the vibrancy of Black churches and schools in the area. In fact, this was one of the main factors that caused St. Peter Claver Catholic School to close.

If there were true allies in diocesan structures, then this pro-life, New Age colonization issue would be addressed, but because many of those in leadership cannot relate to our experience, it is not an issue. Allies are those who are there when the popular attention to an issue has passed but there is still work to be done—especially when there is no attention or benefit to be gained from doing the work or there are negative repercussions from being an ally.

An excellent example of an ally can be found in Fr. Mike, whom I referenced earlier in the book. Fr. Mike was our pastor at St. Peter Claver for nearly three decades. He is a white man from

Maine, studied in Vermont with the Society of St. Edmund, and was trained in Selma, Alabama, to serve and minister *with* the Black community. Yes, there was certainly a learning curve, but Fr. Mike was willing to learn from the community and did not come in a "white savior" to control and "fix" it.

When I started volunteering with the youth group and attending St. Peter Claver for mass during my college years, I was more fully engaged in the well-being of my community, especially the young people God was calling me to serve. During mass, it was not uncommon for Fr. Mike to address the challenges of the Black community in a racist society. On several occasions I heard this white man quote Malcolm X's speech "Who Taught You to Hate Yourself?" Malcolm X delivered that speech during the funeral of Ronald Stokes in Los Angeles in May 1962 to describe our plight and what we were fighting against. Fr. Mike would be sweating and turning red as he exclaimed the words of Malcolm X:

"Who taught you to hate the texture of your hair? Who taught you to hate the color of your skin? To such extent you bleach, to get like the white man. Who taught you to hate the shape of your nose and the shape of your lips? Who taught you to hate yourself from the top of your head to the soles of your feet? Who taught you to hate your own kind? Who taught you to hate the race that you belong to so much so that you don't want to be around each other? . . . You should ask yourself, who taught you to hate being what God made you."

Fr. Mike was asking us to look at society, at a white supremacist society, and what we needed to do to change it. This begins with changing our mindsets, but also being empowered to love who we are as authentic Black people with gifts and talents from our communities. We did not need to seek validation from white people, or white institutions, like the archdiocese, for example, but we needed to be front and center at archdiocesan events to challenge the leadership to see and value us as authentic. This is what is taught at many Black Catholic institutions and organizations around the country.

But the continual challenge is to find our white, Brown, and other allies. They are few and far between for many reasons. One of the main ones can be attributed to the stereotypes that are placed on Blackness that we discussed in the last chapter, and how that permeates the way our church relates to Black people and our institutions.

So, who are our allies? Allies are people

- who listen without judgment and are open to continual learning;
- who are keenly aware of the spaces they occupy where there should be other voices;
- who take the time to educate themselves on the issues and do not always place the burden of education on the community that is affected/vulnerable;
- who learn what is offensive and take action to stop doing offensive things and help others in more dominant groups learn the same;
- who raise up others from marginalized communities to share their own voices in their own authentic ways;
- who create safe spaces for marginalized groups to "vent" and share their challenges without repercussions;
- who believe that the experiences of marginalized groups are genuine and authentic, even though they are not necessarily their own;
- who recognize their own privilege but use it to create opportunities with and for marginalized groups; and

- Who take a stand against racism and other injustices despite the consequences they may face.

I received many threats and accusations when I began advocating for the youth in my community in the Archdiocese of New Orleans, especially after I started doing it for the Black Catholic youth ministry community on a national level after Hurricane Katrina. I have been told that I am not an authentic ministry leader and that I abuse the platform God has given me because I talk too much about "race stuff."

It seems to me that such people do not like to be challenged or made to feel uncomfortable. They want a theology and a spirituality that make them feel happy and content. However, I was raised in a church that taught me, and many like me, to fight against injustices to create the kingdom of heaven here on earth, especially for the most vulnerable. I want a better life with more opportunities afforded to the youth from my community. I want them to have the same fair shot in life as their white counterparts across the country. As a ministry leader knowing that racism is America's "original sin," is it not my responsibility, along with other people of faith, to name it and eradicate it wherever it exists, especially in the church? This is how we level the *praying* field. We must identify the challenges and remove the obstacles. But we have to know our roles in this process and help one another along the way. Only then can we say we are truly one holy body of Christ. Only then can we become the beautiful "gumbo pot" that our wise Creator made us to be.

God bless you as you start to level the *praying* field!

The Game Plan

1. What issues are those who are discriminated against facing in your local community (neighborhood, school, church, elsewhere)?
2. How can you be a better ally, or assist others in being better allies, in addressing the discrimination in your local community?
3. What does a truly holy and just society look like—in the world, in this country, in your local community?

8

Catching
Our Breath

Then he said to me, "Prophesy to these
bones, and say to them: O dry bones,
hear the word of the LORD. Thus says the
LORD GOD to these bones: I will cause
breath to enter you, and you shall live."

—EZEKIEL 37:4-5

One of the most sacred cultural spaces in the United States can be found in my neighborhood of Tremé, Louisiana. Tremé is the oldest Black neighborhood in the United States and has helped shape the Black contribution to the cultural and social fabric of this country. Venerable Mother Henriette Delille, foundress of the Sisters of the Holy Family, of which I am a proud associate member, is also from New Orleans and is the first United States native-born African American whose cause for canonization has been opened by the Catholic Church. She died on November 17, 1862, and her funeral was in Tremé at St. Augustine Church, which was built in 1841 by free people of color so that others, specifically the enslaved Africans of that era, could worship with some form of dignity despite the laws of the time. Tremé was home to Homer Plessy, a Black Catholic parishioner of St. Augustine Church and one of the initial "sparks" of the civil rights movement.

Tremé and the area known as Congo Square is also the birthplace of jazz, one of the most beloved cultural art forms of the United States. Congo Square is a very sacred space in this country, especially to Black people. It is where, even to this day, people gather on Sundays to celebrate culture and pay homage to our ancestors. During the eighteenth century in New Orleans enslaved Africans were commonly "allowed to be off"—I use this phrase with some reservation—on Sundays, as was detailed in the *Code Noir,* which regulated the lives of Black people, specifically the enslaved Africans, of the time. As the slaveowners would gather in the French Quarter on Sundays, many of the enslaved Africans would gather in Congo Square just outside the French Quarter to celebrate their various cultures through song, dance, craftwork, and so on. It was also here that they would interact with free Blacks and the Indigenous of the area, thus creating some of the food, music, celebrations, and my own cultural traditions of the Black Masking/Mardi Gras Indians that much of the world enjoys today when they come to New Orleans. Despite the harsh conditions of the time, it was during this narrow time slot on Sunday afternoons that Black people were allowed to "breathe"—to be their authentic selves where they and their traditions were welcomed or seen as relevant.

Many people, when they visit New Orleans, are unaware of the history and sacred space of Congo Square and are often in awe of these under-told stories. Many continue to be shocked at how little history they know about the city that they are visiting—or may even live in—and the contributions that Black people have made to the culture of the city—then and now. The same misunderstanding of the sacredness of Blackness exists in the wider society today, and specifically in our church. Although there are areas of teaching about our history and contributions, such the Institute for Black Catholic Studies at Xavier University of Louisiana, there has been very little taught about the Black contributions to our faith in our seminaries, higher education institutions, and even religious education programs throughout our parishes. What continues to be taught is the holiness/value of whiteness, and the dismissal/devaluing of Blackness. This bias is evident in various Catholic resources that are published, programs that are aired, and conferences that are held. This sentiment causes many to feel that, if the church does not value Blackness, then why should the wider society?

The questions we need to ask are:

- Is our church, like Congo Square, a safe and sacred place for people of color, specifically Black Catholics, to "breathe"?
- Can Black people express themselves authentically and freely without being scrutinized,

judged, or criticized by other Catholics?

- Can the issues that many of our communities face, such as economic injustice, racism, gentrification, mass incarceration, unequal resources, improper education, police brutality, among others, be deemed relevant pro-life issues in this country since they threaten the quality of life from the womb to the tomb for those in these communities?

About a year has passed since the murder of George Floyd. Many world leaders, including Pope Francis, took notice of, and spoke about, this tragedy and its roots in America's "original sin" of racism. Many white Catholic organizations held webinars and Zoom meetings, doing the best they could during the restrictions caused by the COVID-19 pandemic, to address this issue. Many Black Catholics and other Catholics of color had to take on the unfair but necessary emotional burden to "educate" various Catholic entities about this "original sin" and how it is still present and continues to affect our society and church. As a result, many of us doing this work have received increased criticism, internet trolls, hate mail, and messages by those who think either that we are attacking the church or that racism is a myth. Many have been labeled by various Catholic circles and dioceses as anti-church or as troublemakers. Many of us have had to educate and challenge mostly well-intentioned white colleagues who want to do something about their need to let go of control and let those affected by racism dictate what, how, and when some things should be done. Many of us have had to challenge church structures to ensure that any event, program, or discussion should not center around making white people, or those in power or places of privilege, feel comfortable, but rather should advocate for those on the margins so that there can be true measurable change and that we can hear from, empower, and give resources to those who are directly affected by the issue, thus challenging the "white savior" mentality that so often is brought to such issues.

Fighting this "original sin" has been a painful and long journey for so many, but it has been even more challenging this past year since the murder of George Floyd was witnessed by the world. His final statement, "I can't breathe," which echoes the final statement of many other unarmed black folks who have died at the hands of law enforcement in the past few years, has become one of the many rallying cries for justice globally.

I am part of an informal support group of young lay Black Catholic males involved in ministry that was formed because we could not seem to find authentic support anywhere else in the church. As you may guess, the numbers are low for this group that came together following the murder of George Floyd, mainly because there are so few of us who fit the category of young, lay, Black, and male in Catholic ministry. We have been trying to figure out how we can "breathe"—be our authentic Black Catholic selves in our own church without being seen as "unholy" or a "threat." We are exhausted by not being valued or seen by our own church. We are tired of feeling unsafe in a church where we so often have to defend our involvement in the church within our own community and fight those who see us as a threat, simply because we are advocating for our own community.

Therefore, what can the church and our allies along this journey do? *Let the church breathe!* Let the Holy Spirit, *the breath of God*, flow throughout our church and society to create hope and healing where it is needed. We have found hope and healing breath in those bishops and church leaders who are open to and understand that saying "*Black lives matter*" is not an endorsement of an organization but the affirmation of a group of people who have been continually attacked and marginalized throughout the history of this country. We have found hope and healing breath in those Catholic spaces where we see white Catholics, and those in places of privilege or power, grappling with and trying to dismantle racism, white supremacy, biased thinking, and other divisions within their parishes and organizations. We experience hope and healing breath when our brothers and sisters of various races, most recently our Asian/Pacific Islander brothers and sisters who have also experienced racist attacks since the pandemic started, finally accept our problems as authentic problems that deserve attention and work not *for* but *with* our communities who have traditionally been ignored or left to fend for themselves in order to create both effective and mutually beneficial relationships and change. We have experienced hope and healing breath in spaces where we have seen dioceses take a "racism inventory" of their structure and operations and work to divert resources to make amends for past systemic racism that they may have participated in and perpetuated. We have experienced hope and healing breath when we have seen our church leadership working with local law enforcement to address the needed change, not to attack officers, but to address the broken justice system that has perpetuated the unchecked violence in so many communities of color.

Personally, my breath—a physical expression of my emotional state—was stifled as the jury in the Derek Chauvin trial went into deliberation. I was honestly shocked at their guilty verdict because of past decisions of trials involving white law enforcement using lethal force against unarmed citizens, especially unarmed Black citizens. Although I was able to breathe a little, I am still cautious about other repercussions occurring in response to the trial and any changes that may occur afterward due to the verdict.

Of course, true justice would mean that George Floyd would still be alive today. Therefore, I view the verdict as a form of accountability rather than justice being served. Yes, there is still much work to do, and I believe much can be done in, and through, the church. We have the documents, and we have the roadmap of how we are all, as the *Catechism of the Catholic Church* states, "made in the image and likeness of God" (no. 1934). We just have to be humble; learn more about and accept each other's cultures, sacred spaces, values, traditions; and see our unique needs as equally valuable and holy as anyone else's. It is then we, as a church, will become that sacred and safe space to allow the Holy Spirit to *breathe* life and healing into this—sometimes suffocating—body of faith.

The Game Plan

1. What has this book challenged, or affirmed in, me to do in order to level the praying field for my community and world?

Afterword

Bishop Fernand J. Cheri III, OFM

Auxiliary Bishop of the Archdiocese of New Orleans

If anybody ask you who I am,
Who I am, who I am,
If anybody ask you who I am,
Tell them I'm a child of God

"Tell Them I'm a Child of God" is one of my favorite spirituals that I sing for confirmations. It prompts the assembly to remember that our discipleship in Jesus calls us to affirm we are all God's children, coheirs to God's riches, blessings, grace, and mercy. That is the very thing that racism takes away when it shows its ugly face.

When we read this book, we are called to reflect on our true, radically centered identity as children of God, and therefore not to be misshaped or deformed by the world's efforts to devalue or deny us our full humanity and freedom. We connect to this text by looking at our past and learning how to deal with our present, so that we can better shape our future.

One of my most memorable racist encounters happened in the seminary. We were taking an introduction to sociology course, and we got to the chapter on Blacks and Hispanics. The instructor, the vice-rector of the seminary, said that we were going to skip this chapter and take it up in next semester's course. That course was entitled "Deviants." I almost went ballistic. I got more enraged as he and others could not understand my objection. I was resolved to prove him wrong. Now, some fifty years later, I realize what a waste of my time, energy, and life itself it was to try and educate all those involved. Enraged, labeled, and debased, I felt stressed, almost paralyzed, by this perspective until I resolved that I couldn't fix him or others like him; only God could do that.

"Open Wide Our Hearts," the 2018 pastoral letter by the United States Conference of Catholic Bishops (USCCB), calls racism America's original sin and evil. Systemic racism is an immoral monster. The root problem is our incapacity to confront this brutal immoral monster that violates Black people and people of color. Does not the fact that racism infects every piece of our past and present make it a Catholic issue that needs a Catholic God, a Catholic people, and a Catholic prayer? The immoral monster lives in us, but so does the revolutionary love of Jesus Christ. Child of God, where do you stand? Is it in solidarity with the *church on the margins*, or do you hold them in contempt?

Child of God, do you profess and confess your complicity with racism in your silence? Are you living in denial, turning a blind eye to the racist political upheaval of January 6, 2021, on the US Capitol? The conviction of Derek Chauvin is not enough. The violence against Black bodies and people of color still permeates the American landscape and the Catholic Church. Lord, have mercy!

Child of God, can you keep your hand on the gospel plow and hold on, keep the faith and run the race? We are living in challenging times, just like in ages past. So what is new? Is not the Spirit of God upon you to bring glad tidings to the lowly, to heal the broken hearts of the marginalized?

I must confess that I am still learning the scope of racism in society and in the church. I am troubled by our failures to march for racial justice today. I confess that I can never do enough to promote Black Lives Matter as a Right to Life mantra and a principle of Catholic social teaching, second to none.

I confess that I have not been a voice for justice in the past. I thank God for putting me in situations and before people who awaken me to my calling. I may not be all that I should be, but thank God, I ain't what I was. I am on the battlefield for my Lord, determined not to let racism go unchallenged.

I have learned that living in denial of racism gives you a heart attack. You are plagued by racism's theft of your God-given inheritance and dignity. Racism eats away the fabric of your self-esteem and fills you with rage. Therefore, you must take a stand and take action. I have learned it the hard way. As preacher and professor Jeremiah Wright once said, "Everybody your color is not your kind, and everybody your kind is not your color!" You have to work on being of the same mind and culture and gospel values. Assumptions make fools of us all.

There are over four hundred bishops in the United States and the Virgin Islands. I am one of only six active and five retired Black Catholic bishops in the United States. It is foolhardy to assume that combatting racism will be a top priority in the church, equal to abortion. Yet I cannot give up the fight to push for racial equity and justice. That is why before the 2017 Convocation of Catholic Diocesan Leaders in Florida, I told the planners and the whole USCCB that among the sixty-six workshops planned on the theme of missionary discipleship, none offered anything for me as a Black Catholic, or addressed the values of people of color that can enrich the Catholic Church and its mission in Jesus Christ. I felt a need to hold us accountable to this truth.

My hope is built on nothing less than Jesus's love and righteousness. In the old days in the confirmation rite, after the bishop anointed you saying, "Be sealed in the gift of the Holy Spirit," he would gently slap you and say, "Peace be with you!" The idea behind that gesture was to remind you that a confirmed Catholic is a champion for Christ and must be about the mission of Jesus—to wake up and make it real. I tell the confirmandi: "I am tempted to slap you, but I won't! But show and tell the world that you are a child of God."

Appendix 1

Catholic Resources

Vatican Council II,
Gaudium et Spes,
1965

Discrimination

With respect to the fundamental rights of the person, every type of discrimination, whether social or cultural, whether based on sex, race, color, social condition, language or religion, is to be overcome and eradicated as contrary to God's intent. . . . The equal dignity of persons demands that a more humane and just condition of life be brought about. For excessive economic and social differences between the members of the one human family or population groups cause scandal, and militate against social justice, equity, the dignity of the human person, as well as social and international peace (no. 29).

Catechism of the Catholic Church, **1992**

Equality

Created in the image of the one God and equally endowed with rational souls, all men have the same nature and the same origin. Redeemed by the sacrifice of Christ, all are called to participate in the same divine beatitude: all therefore enjoy an equal dignity. The equality of men rests essentially on their dignity as persons and the rights that flow from it: Every form of social or cultural discrimination in fundamental personal rights on the grounds of sex, race, color, social conditions, language, or religion must be curbed and eradicated as incompatible with God's design (nos. 1934, 1935)

Pope Francis,
World Day of Migrants and Refugees,
2019

Racism

The problem is not that we have doubts and fears. The problem is when they condition our way of thinking and acting to the point of making us intolerant, closed and perhaps even—without realizing it—racist. In this way, fear deprives us of the desire and the ability to encounter the other, the person different from myself; it deprives me of an opportunity to encounter the Lord.

USCCB,
Brothers and Sisters to Us,
1979

Racism

Racism is a sin: a sin that divides the human family, blots out the image of God among specific members of that family, and violates the fundamental human dignity of those called to be children of the same Father. . . . It mocks the words of Jesus: "Treat others the way you would have them treat you." Indeed, racism is more than a disregard for the words of Jesus; it is a denial of the truth of the dignity of each human being revealed by the mystery of the Incarnation.

Many times the new face of racism is the computer print-out, the graph of profits and losses, the pink slip, the nameless statistic. Today's racism flourishes in the triumph of private concern over public responsibility, individual success over social commitment, and personal fulfillment over authentic compassion.

Let the Church proclaim to all that the sin of racism defiles the image of God and degrades the sacred dignity of humankind which has been revealed by the mystery of the Incarnation. Let all know that it is a terrible sin that mocks the cross of Christ and ridicules the Incarnation. For the brother and sister of our Brother Jesus Christ are brother and sister to us.

Racism and economic oppression are distinct but interrelated forces which dehumanize our society. Movement toward authentic justice demands a simultaneous attack on both evils.

The difficulties of these new times demand a new vision and a renewed courage to transform our society and achieve justice for all. We must fight for the dual goals of racial and economic justice with determination and creativity.

There must be no turning back along the road of justice, not sighing for bygone times of privilege, no nostalgia for simple solutions from another age. For we are the children of the age to come, when the first shall be last and the last shall be first, when blessed are they who serve Christ the Lord in all His brothers and sisters, especially those who are poor and suffer injustice.

Racism is not merely one sin among many; it is a radical evil that divides the human family and denies the new creation of a redeemed world. To struggle against it demands an equally radical transformation, in our own minds and hearts as well as in the structure of our society.

The new forms of racism must be brought face-to-face with the figure of Christ. It is Christ's word that is the judgment on this world; it is Christ's cross that is the measure of our response; and it is Christ's face that is the composite of all persons but in a most significant way of today's poor, today's marginal people, today's minorities.

Social Justice

Each of us as Catholics must acknowledge a share in the mistakes and sins of the past. Many of us have been prisoners of fear and prejudice. We have preached the Gospel while closing our eyes to the racism it condemns. We have allowed conformity to social pressures to replace compliance with social justice.

US Black Catholic Bishops, *What We Have Seen and Heard,* 1984

Social Justice

We oppose all oppression and all injustice, for unless all are free, none are free. Moreover, oppression by some means freedom's destruction for both the oppressor and the oppressed, and liberation liberates the oppressor and the oppressed.

Pontifical Commission on Justice and Peace, *The Church and Racism: Towards a More Fraternal Society,* 1988

Discrimination

Man's creation by God 'in his own image' confers upon every human person an eminent dignity; it also postulates the fundamental equality of all human beings. For the Church, this equality, which is rooted in man's being, acquires the dimension of an altogether special brotherhood through the Incarnation of the Son of God. . . . In the Redemption effected by Jesus Christ the Church sees a further basis of the rights and duties of the human person. Hence every form of discrimination based on race . . . is absolutely unacceptable (no. 17).

Social Justice

This principle of the equal dignity of all persons, of whatever race, already finds solid support in the sciences and a firm basis in philosophy, ethics and religions in general. The Christian faith respects this intuition, this affirmation, and rejoices in it. It represents a considerable convergence among the various disciplines which reinforces the convictions of the majority of people of good will and allows the drawing up of universal declarations, conventions and international agreements for the protection of human rights, and the elimination of all forms of racial discrimination (no. 18).

Racism

Faith in the one God, Creator and Redeemer of all humankind made in his image and likeness, constitutes the absolute and inescapable negation of any racist ideologies. It is still necessary to draw out all the consequences of this: "We cannot truly pray to God the Father of all if we treat any people in other than brotherly fashion, for all men are created in God's image" (no. 19).

Doctrine and examples by themselves are not sufficient. The victims of racism, wherever they may be, must be defended. Acts of discrimination among persons and peoples for racist or other reasons—religious or ideological—and which lead to contempt and to the phenomena of exclusion, must be denounced and brought to light without hesitation and strongly rejected in order to promote equitable behavior, legislative dispositions and social structures (no. 26).

The 1965 UN Convention expressed this conviction forcefully: 'Any doctrine of superiority based on the difference between races is scientifically false, morally condemnable and socially unjust and dangerous.' The Church's doctrine affirms it with no less vigor: all racist theories are contrary to Christian faith and love. And yet, in sharp contrast to this growing awareness of human dignity, racism still exists and continually reappears in different forms. It is a wound in humanity's side that mysteriously remains open. Everyone, therefore, must make efforts to heal it with great firmness and patience (no. 33).

Equality

The Second Vatican Council has rightly defined the Church as "sacrament, a sign and instrument, that is, of communion with God and of unity among all men" since "both Christ and the Church . . . transcend the distinctions of race and nationality." Within the Church "no inequality arising from race or nationality, social condition or sex" should exist. This is indeed the meaning of the word "Catholic"—i.e., universal, which is one of the marks of the Church. As the Church spreads, this catholicity becomes more manifest (no. 22).

Equality does not mean uniformity. It is important to recognize the diversity and complementarity of one another's cultural riches and moral qualities. Equality of treatment therefore implies a certain recognition of differences which minorities themselves demand in order to develop according to their own specific characteristics, in respect for others and for the common good of society and the world community. No human group, however, can boast of having a natural superiority over others, or of exercising any discrimination that affects the basic rights of the person (no. 23).

USCCB,
Open Wide Our Hearts,
2018

Racism

Racism can often be found in our hearts—in many cases placed there unwillingly or unknowingly by our upbringing and culture. As such, it can lead to thoughts and actions that we do not even see as racist, but nonetheless flow from the same prejudicial root. Racism can also be institutional, when practices or traditions are upheld that treat certain groups of people unjustly. The cumulative effects of personal sins of racism have led to social structures of injustice and violence that make us all accomplices in racism (no. 5).

Reform

All of us are in need of personal, ongoing conversion. Our churches and our civic and social institutions are in need of ongoing reform. If racism is confronted by addressing its causes and the injustice it produces, then healing can occur (no. 7).

———

**Pope Francis,
World Youth Day Vigil,
July 30, 2016**

Youth

Life nowadays tells us that it is much easier to concentrate on what divides us, what keeps us apart. People try to make us believe that being closed in on ourselves is the best way to keep safe from harm. Today, we adults need you to teach us, as you are doing today, how to live in diversity, in dialogue, to experience multiculturalism, not as a threat but an opportunity. You are an opportunity for the future.

Appendix 2

Ten Important Statistics of the United States

1. The 2019 demographic breakdown of the US population: 60.1 percent is White; 18.5 percent is Hispanic; 12.2 percent is Black; 5.6 percent is Asian; 0.7 percent is Native American; 0.2 percent is Native Hawaiian or other Pacific Islander; and 2.8 percent is of multiple races.[1]

2. Of the 532 voting members of Congress, 59 are Black, 46 are Hispanic, 17 are Asian American, and 6 are Native American.[2]

3. Of the state prison population in the United States, 38 percent is Black, 35 percent is White, and

---

[1] Iman Ghosh, "Visualizing the US Population by Race," *Visual Capitalist*, December 28, 2020.

[2] Katherine Schaeffer, "Racial, Ethnic Diversity Increases Yet Again with the 117th Congress," Pew Research Center, January 28, 2021.

21 percent is Hispanic. Blacks are imprisoned at five times the rate of Whites.[3]

4. In 2016, 35 percent of Whites had a college degree, compared to 21 percent of Blacks and 15 percent of Hispanics.[4]

5. In the US, 18.8 percent of the Black population and 15.7 percent of the Hispanic population live in poverty, compared to 7.3 percent of Whites.[5]

6. In 2018, the average Black worker earned only 62 percent of the amount earned by the average White worker.[6]

7. In the second quarter of 2020, the unemployment rate was 12 percent for Whites, 16.1 percent for Blacks, 14.3 percent for Asians, and 16.7 percent

[3] Ashley Nellis, PhD, *The Color of Justice: Racial and Ethnic Disparity in State Prisons*, The Sentencing Project, June 14, 2016.

[4] "Indicator 27: Educational Attainment," National Center for Education Statistics, updated February 2019.

[5] "Poverty Rate by Race and Hispanic Origin: 1959 to 2019," US Census Bureau, September 2020.

[6] Shayanne Gal, Andy Kiersz, Michelle Mark, Ruobing Su, and Marguerite Ward, "26 Simple Charts to Show Friends and Family Who Aren't Convinced Racism Is Still a Problem in America," *Insider*, July 8, 2020.

for Hispanics. Twelve months later, in the second quarter of 2021, the unemployment rate was 5.1 percent for Whites, 9.2 percent for Blacks, 5.6 percent for Asians, and 7.2 percent for Hispanics.[7]

8. In the second quarter of 2019, the homeownership rate for White households was 73.1 percent, compared to 46.6 percent for Hispanic households and 40.6 percent for Black households.[8]

9. In 2019, the median income was $76,057 for White households, $46,073 for Black households, and $56,113 for Hispanic households.[9]

10. In 2019, 20 percent of Hispanics and 11.4 percent of Blacks lacked health insurance, compared to 7.8 percent of Whites.[10]

---

[7] US Bureau of Labor Statistics, "Labor Force Statistics from the Current Population Survey," July 2, 2021.

[8] Andrew Haughwout, Donghoon Lee, Joelle Scally, and Wilbert van der Klaauw, "Inequality in US Homeownership Rates by Race and Ethnicity," *Liberty Street Economics* (blog), July 8, 2020.

[9] Valerie Wilson, "Racial Disparities in Income and Poverty Remain Largely Unchanged amid Strong Income Growth in 2019," *Working Economics Blog*, September 16, 2020.

[10] "Uninsured Rates for the Nonelderly by Race/Ethnicity," State Health Facts, KFF (Kaiser Family Foundation), 2019.

Appendix 3

A Prayer Service for Black Children of God

The prayer begins with the Sign of the Cross.

SIGN OF THE CROSS AND LITURGICAL GREETING

Presider: In the name of the Father, and of the Son, and of the Holy Spirit.

All: Amen.

The presider, extending his hands, greets the people, saying:

Presider: The grace of our Lord Jesus Christ and the love of God, and the communion of the Holy Spirit be with you all.

All: And with your Spirit

This is an adaptation of "Requiem for Black Children of God," which was created in 2020 by Bishop Fernand Cheri of the Archdiocese of New Orleans.

Presider: As the Body of Christ, let us go into the streets proclaiming our solidarity with those who have died unjustly.

PENITENTIAL ACT

Presider: Brothers and sisters, let us acknowledge our sins,

and so prepare ourselves to confess our omissions.

(*A moment of silent reflection follows.*)

All: I confess to almighty God
and to you, my brothers and sisters,
that I have greatly sinned,
in my thoughts and in my words,
in what I have done and in what I
have failed to do,

(*And, striking their breasts and the gong rings three times, they say:*)

through my fault, through my fault,
through my most grievous fault;
therefore I ask blessed Mary ever-
Virgin,
all the Angels and Saints,
and you, my brothers and sisters,
to pray for me to the Lord our God.

Presider: May Almighty God have mercy on us, forgive us our sins, and bring us to everlasting life.

All: Amen.

OPENING PRAYER

Presider: Let us pray

(Silence.)

O God, author of true freedom,

whose will it is to shape all men and women

into a single people released from slavery,

and who offer us a tome of grace and blessing,

grant to your people, we pray,

that, as we receive new growth in freedom,

we may appear more clearly to the world

as the universal sacrament of salvation,

manifesting and making present

the mystery of your love for all.

Through our Lord Jesus Christ, your Son,

who lives and reigns with you

in the unity of the Holy Spirit,
one God, forever and ever.

All: **Amen.**

READING   Isaiah 61:1

(The reader goes to the podium.)

Reader: A reading from the Book of the Prophet Isaiah.

For Zion's sake I will not be silent,
for Jerusalem's sake I will not be quiet,
until her vindication goes forth like the dawn,
and her victory like a burning torch.

The Word of the Lord.

All: **Thanks be to God.**

The reader returns to his or her place.
All then sing a hymn in response, such as "Balm in Gilead."

GOSPEL   Matthew 5:13–16

The deacon then proclaims the Gospel from the podium.

Deacon: The Lord be with you.

All: **And with your spirit**

Deacon: A reading from the holy Gospel according to Matthew.

Jesus said to his disciples:

"You are the salt of the earth.
But if salt loses its taste, with what can
it be seasoned?
It is no longer good for anything,
but to be thrown out and trampled under-
foot.
"You are the light of the world.
A city set on a mountain cannot be hidden.
Nor do they light a lamp
and then put it under a bushel basket;
it is set on a lampstand,
where it gives light to all in the house.
Just so, let your light shine before others,
that they may see your good deeds,
and glorify your heavenly Father."
The Gospel of the Lord.

All: **Praise to you Lord, Jesus Christ.**

REFLECTION
S's to the Third Power
Isaiah 62:1; Matthew 5:13-16
Let us be clear, Jesus doesn't say we used to be,
we ought to be, or we are going to be. No, he
states unmistakably and simply that we are the
salt, the city, and the light. Did he not? True to
this call today, we have assembled in a state of

unrest as we watch with horror the events unfolding across these United States and the world. It is clear that people of all generations, languages, and ways of life have taken to the streets to protest the killing of another Black man by law enforcement. Enough is enough; this scene drains our spirits and clouds the union of the human family. As toxic as the crossroads of life are these days, will we have the courage and wisdom to stay vigilant amid this pandemic and the gross violence and abuse by law enforcement? This is not a time for the faint of heart, but for the courageous.

Stand Up . . .

- We are the salt of righteousness, that preservative which raises blood pressure. We are the salt of righteousness, standing with those championing freedom and equality in peaceful demonstration. We must stand up for freedom. We cannot rest but must fight against authoritarian regimes that stifle our freedom of speech guaranteed in our Constitution.

- We are a city on a hill, a city of justice shining brightly as a metropolis of integrity and familial comradeship. We must stand up as a community against the corruptive forces of evil, a body against over four hundred years of systematic racism—slavery, lynching, civil war, Jim Crow laws, segregation, unlawful policing and inequality.

- We are the light of truth that cannot be ignored or hidden but gives sight to all humanity. We must stand up and profess that human dignity and value at every level is the true issue of right to life. We must stand up against these inhuman acts as our forbearers struggled, bleed, and died in exposing lost moral authority and respect.

Stand Up . . .

- I do what I can when I can while I can for my people.
- Don't let their names be forgotten for Black Lives Matter.
- There is a balm in Gilead, a medicine used in bible days to heal the sin-sick soul and make the wounded whole.
- For I can't breathe, because my God-given breath of life is being taken from me.
- My brother has a knee on his neck. Am I not my brother's keeper?

Speak Up . . .

True prophets, called by God, spoke up warning their people that rebelling against the covenant—the promises that God made to them and that they made to God—would lead to the destruction of the nation and would lead to their exile from their own best hopes and dreams. Isaiah was the eagle-eyed prophet who contemplated the sins of the people and called forth a new vision of God's truth and morality. Isaiah did not preach because he had to say something, but rather because he had something to say. Not saying it—would have destroyed him!

> For Zion's sake I will not be silent,
> For Jerusalem's sake I will not be
>   quiet.

I will not be silent. I will not be quiet.

We can't afford to be silent any longer . . .

- For Black, Brown and people of color are trapped in the net of a system that has smothered the lives of too many of our sons and daughters.
- For George Floyd now joins a refrain of voices crying out from the grave.

- For the countless George Floyds whose lives have been snuffed out prematurely.
- Say their names, tell the story for Black Lives Matter.
- The dehumanization of African Americans and people of color must come to an end.
- Do what we can when we can while we can for all people.
- For the promises of God still have their day.

Sit Down . . .

This is not meant to be an insult to anyone; however let's be clear. It's not about me. It's not about you. It's about the Lord.

Today, we acknowledge those who have died unjustly. We say their names for their victimization and horrific deaths disturb our peace.

We can't do enough . . .

- To encourage law enforcement to apply same standards to all people.
- To show that being Black should not be a crime in America or in the world.
- To join peace-loving people to eliminate centuries of institutional racism.

Does anyone here remember when wrestling was at its zenith? There were tag-team matches. The only way to enter the match was to be tagged by your partner. It's time to sit down and tag in our great God—Father, Son, and Holy Spirit—and let him bring us home.

I must confess, "I will not be silent." AMEN.
A short period of silence follows the reflection.

READING OF NAMES
Presider: Brothers and sisters,
the scars of systematic racism plague our nation,
our communities and our churches.
For too long,
too many of us stood silent or said too little
as our Black brothers and sisters
succumbed by the brutal blows
of racism's cruel injustice.
Let us say their names,
those who bled and died on this punishing cross
and ask forgiveness.
The names are read, alternating readers.
As a name is proclaimed, the gong is stroked and the people respond:
All: **Forgive us, we pray.**

Reader 1	Reader 2	Reader 3
Rodney King	Amadou Diallo	Sean Bell
Oscar Grant	Malice Green	Abner Louima
Trayvon Martin	Freddie Gray	Nathaniel Edwards
Rekia Boyd	Rafael Cruz	Harith Augustus
Michael Brown	Kajuan Raye	Botham Jean
Laquan McDonald	Paul O'Neal	Isiah Murrietta-
Tamir Rice	Alton Sterling	Golding
Eric Garner	Philando Castile	Antwan Rose II
Sandra Bland	Terence Crutcher	O'Shae Terry
Bettie Jones	Devaris "Caine"	Devon Bailey
Quintonio LeGrier	Rogers	Atatiana Jefferson
Walter Scott	Stephon Clark	Kenneth French
Eric Harris	Juan Flores	Michael Dean
Tony Robinson	Marco Gomez	Bruce Carter
Rumain Brisbon	Eddie Lee	Genevive Dawes
Breonna Taylor	Patterson	Ahmaud Arbery
George Floyd	Gus Tousis	Aiyana Jones
	John Crawford	
	Duante Wright	

After all have been read, the gong is rung three times as all remain silent.
Then the presider offers the closing prayer.

CLOSING PRAYER
Presider: O God,
              forgive us for being a party to injustice
              in the lives of these your children,
              our Black sisters and brothers,

and all victims of systemic racism
in these United States.
Forgive us for not seeing them as coheirs
to life,
liberty and the pursuit of happiness.
Forgive us for not hearing their cries,
"I CAN'T BREATHE" or
"HANDS UP, DON'T SHOOT."
Forgive us for not lifting them up as
your children,
precious in your sight.
Increase our strength, we pray, O Lord,
that we may drink deeply of love's
power
and everywhere promote your justice
and peace.
Through Christ our Lord.

All: **Amen.**

Presider: At the Savior's command
and formed by the Word of God, we dare
to say:

All: Our Father . . .

Presider: The Lord be with you.

All: **And with your spirit.**

Presider: May almighty God bless us,
protect us from all evil
and bring us to everlasting life.

All: **Amen.**

Presider: Go in peace.

All: **Thanks be to God.**